Anonymous

Tales of Adventure and Stories of Travel

of Fifty Years Ago

Anonymous

Tales of Adventure and Stories of Travel
of Fifty Years Ago

ISBN/EAN: 9783744750721

Printed in Europe, USA, Canada, Australia, Japan

Cover: Foto ©Andreas Hilbeck / pixelio.de

More available books at **www.hansebooks.com**

THE COUNTESS OF BLESSINGTON.

By E. T. Parris.

TALES OF ADVENTURE

AND

STORIES OF TRAVEL

OF FIFTY YEARS AGO

ILLUSTRATED WITH TWENTY PLATES
FROM 'THE ANNUALS'

LONDON
SAMPSON LOW, MARSTON AND COMPANY
LIMITED
St. Dunstan's House
FETTER LANE, FLEET STREET, E.C.
1893

All rights reserved

PREFACE

THESE TALES OF ADVENTURE AND STORIES OF TRAVEL have been gleaned from many volumes of the 'Annuals' which were so much the rage between fifty and sixty years ago. Although there was much that was trivial in them, and amateur writers rather than literary men filled most of the pages with their contributions, yet among the three hundred volumes that were published between the years 1823 and 1850 there were sure to be some literary efforts deserving of a better fate than to be buried with the rest.

And in my endeavour to select some of the worthiest of these stories I have found that the personal accounts of travels and a few historical tales have been the best written and most interesting. I have added a few pages of poetry, though these, I must confess, were chosen more to explain the accompanying plates than for any other reason.

And it is of these plates I would say a few words. If on no other account, the editors of the 'Annuals' demand our cordial thanks, since everyone must acknowledge that they raised the standard of copperplate engraving (or, rather, engraving on steel) from a very low point to, we may say, the acme of perfection. We shall never see again such a work as 'The Crucifixion,' engraved by H. Le Keux, after John Martin; or the 'Rouen,' by W. Miller, or 'Lake Nemi,' by J. Cousen, after Turner: even the painter himself—grumbler as he was—acknowledged their excellence. From a hundred to a hundred and eighty pounds were paid to Le Keux and the other artists for engraving these little plates, no larger than your hand, and they were well worth the money. Some day proof impressions of these splendid examples of a nearly lost art will be sought for by collectors, as Rembrandt etchings are at the present day. Many efforts were made to find the original steel-plates on which these engravings were made—unfortunately, with little success. It appears that most of them were sold for exportation to America and Australia.

In order to preserve a record of the 'Annuals,' I give a list, nearly perfect, of all that were published.

J. C.

THE ANNUALS

THEIR EDITORS AND THEIR PUBLISHERS

THE FORGET-ME-NOT. 1823–1847.
    Edited by H. Shoberl. *Published by* Rudolph Ackermann.

FRIENDSHIP'S OFFERING. 1824–1844.
    Edited by T. Pringle and others. *Published by* Smith & Elder.

LITERARY SOUVENIR: CABINET OF MODERN ART. 1825–1837.
    Edited by Alaric Watts. *Published by* Longmans and others.

THE AMULET. 1826–1837.
    Edited by S. C. Hall. *Published by* Westley & Davis.

THE BIJOU. 1828–1830.
    Edited by Sir Harris Nicolas (?). *Published by* W. Pickering.

WINTER'S WREATH. 1828–1832.
    Edited by George Smith. *Published by* G. Smith.

THE KEEPSAKE. 1828–1857.
    Edited by the Countess of Blessington and others. *Published by* Longmans and David Bogue.

THE ANNIVERSARY. 1829.
    Edited by Allan Cunningham. *Published by* John Sharpe.

THE TALISMAN. 1829.
    Edited by Elam Bliss. *Published by* Bliss (N. Y.).

THE GEM. 1829–1832.
  Edited by W. Marshall (?). *Published by* W. Marshall.

THE IRIS. 1830.
  Edited by Rev. T. Dale. *Published by* Sampson Low.

LANDSCAPE ANNUAL. 1830–1839.
  Edited by Thomas Roscoe. *Published by* Jennings & Chaplin.

HOOD'S COMIC ANNUAL. 1830–1839, and 1842.
  Edited by T. Hood. *Published by* A. H. Baily and others.

THE CAMEO. 1831.
  Edited by W. Pickering. *Published by* Pickering.

THE REMEMBRANCE. 1831.
  Edited by T. Roscoe. *Published by* Jennings & Chaplin.

THE TALISMAN. 1831.
  Edited by Zillah Watts. *Published by* Whittaker & Co.

THE COMIC OFFERING. 1831–1832.
  Edited by Louisa H. Sheridan. *Published by* Smith & Elder.

THE BOTANIC ANNUAL. 1832.
  Edited by Robert Mudie. *Published by* Cochrane.

THE AMETHYST. 1832–1834.
  Edited by Dr. Hine. *Published by* Oliphant.

THE EASTER OFFERING. 1832.
  Edited by Joseph Booker. *Published by* Booker.

PICTURESQUE ANNUAL. 1832–1845.
  Edited by Leitch Ritchie. *Published by* Longman & Co.

DRAWING-ROOM SCRAP-BOOK. 1832–1852.
  Edited by L. E. L. and others. *Published by* Fisher & Co.

AURORA BOREALIS. 1833.
  Edited by W. Howitt. *Published by* Empson.

LANDSCAPE ALBUM. 1833–1834.
  Edited by Charles Tilt. *Published by* C. Tilt.

TURNER'S ANNUAL TOUR. 1833–1835.
    Edited by Leitch Ritchie. *Published by* Longman & Co.

THE CHRISTIAN KEEPSAKE. 1833–1840.
    Edited by Rev. W. Ellis. *Published by* Fisher & Co.

THE BOOK OF BEAUTY. 1833–1849.
    Edited by the Countess of Blessington and others. *Published by* Longman & Co.

THE ORIENTAL ANNUAL. 1834–1840.
    Edited by Rev. Hobart Caunter. *Published by* Bull & Churton.

LANDSCAPE WREATH. 1835 (?).
    Edited by Thomas Campbell. *Published by* G. Virtue.

GEMS OF BEAUTY. (4to.) 1836–1840.
    Edited by the Countess of Blessington. *Published by* Longman & Co.

CONTINENTAL LANDSCAPE ANNUAL. 1837–1838.
    Edited by F Fergusson. *Published by* H. Riley.

FINDEN'S TABLEAUX. (4to.) 1837–1844.
    Edited by Miss Mitford and others. *Published by* Tilt.

THE HUNTERS' ANNUAL. 1838–1839.
    Edited by A. H. Baily. *Published by* A. H. Baily & Co.

CHILDREN OF THE NOBILITY. (4to.) 1838–1841.
    Edited by Mrs. Fairlie. *Published by* Hogarth (?).

FLOWERS OF LOVELINESS. (4to.) 1838–1841.
    Edited by (?). *Published by* Ackermann & Co.

PORTRAITS OF THE FEMALE ARISTOCRACY. (4to.) 1840–1841.
    Edited by W. Finden. *Published by* Hogarth.

THE PROTESTANT ANNUAL. 1841.
    Edited by Charlotte Elizabeth. *Published by* Baisler.

THE CORONAL. 1846.
    Edited by E. Lacey. *Published by* Lacey.

THE AMARANTH. (4to.) 1859.
    Edited by T. K. Hervey. *Published by* A. H. Baily & Co.

JUVENILE ANNUALS

JUVENILE FORGET-ME-NOT. 1828–1831.
    Edited by Mrs. S. C. Hall. *Published by* Westley.

JUVENILE KEEPSAKE. 1829–1830.
    Edited by T. Roscoe. *Published by* Hurst & Co.

CHRISTMAS-BOX. 1830–1831.
    Edited by W. Marshall. *Published by* Marshall.

JUVENILE FORGET-ME-NOT. 1830–1835.
    Edited by H. Shoberl. *Published by* Ackermann.

THE EXCITEMENT. 1830–1845.
    Edited by Rev. R. Jamieson. *Published by* Waugh & Innes.

JUVENILE SCRAP-BOOK. 1836–1850.
    Edited by Agnes Strickland. *Published by* Fisher & Son.

CONTENTS

	PAGE
PREFACE. *By the Editor*	v
THE ANNUALS; THEIR EDITORS AND THEIR PUBLISHERS	vii
THE ENTRY OF EDWARD THE BLACK PRINCE INTO LONDON. *By Sir Harris Nicolas*	1
THE GARDEN OF BOCCACIO. *By S. T. Coleridge*	12
THE FAMILY OF SIR THOMAS MORE	16
THE DEATH OF THE REGENT MURRAY. *By Sir Walter Scott*	29
THE PALACE OF JUSTICE, BRUGES. *By Thomas Roscoe*	38
ON A LADY PLAYING THE GUITAR. *By Barry Cornwall*	44
NOTES OF A SPANISH RAMBLE, IN THE SUMMER OF 1839. *By Lord John Manners*	45
THE PLAZA REAL AND THE CATHEDRAL, SEVILLE, WITH THE PROCESSION OF THE CORPUS CHRISTI CEREMONY. *By Thomas Roscoe*	68
ARAB THIEVES. *From Adventures of Giovanni Finati, translated by W. J. Bankes*	71
THE FAMILY OF SIR WALTER SCOTT. *Letter from Sir Walter Scott to Sir Adam Ferguson*	76
THE LADY'S DREAM. *A Spanish Serenade*	80
TO BE READ AT DUSK. *By Charles Dickens*	81
LAKE NEMI. *By Lord Byron*	96
NARRATIVE OF AN ASCENT OF MONT BLANC IN AUGUST, 1830. *By the Hon. E. B. Wilbraham*	98

CONTENTS

	PAGE
HAPPY ANGLERS. *By W. M. Thackeray*	115
AN ADVENTURE IN SPAIN. *By J. B.*	117
THE NUPTIALS OF THE DOGE OF VENICE WITH THE ADRIATIC SEA. *By Lord Morpeth*	138
ORIENTAL SPORTS. *By the Rev. Hobart Caunter, B.D.*	142
THE STORM. *By Adelaide Anne Procter*	151
AN INTERESTING EVENT. *By W. M. Thackeray*	153
A SUMMER DAY. *By J. Dodds*	162
ROUEN—FROM ST. CATHERINE'S HILL. *By J. C.*	166
WILLIAM COLLINS, R.A. *By Richard Redgrave, R.A.*	168
LETITIA ELIZABETH LANDON. *By William Howitt*	174
THE COUNTESS OF BLESSINGTON	178
THE RIVER LOIRE AND THE CITY OF TOURS. *By J. C.*	180

LIST OF THE PLATES

THE COUNTESS OF BLESSINGTON (see page 178). From a drawing by E. T. Parris	Frontispiece
THE ENTRY OF THE BLACK PRINCE INTO LONDON. From a drawing by F. P. Stephanoff	To face p. 9
THE GARDEN OF BOCCACIO. From the painting by T. Stothard, R.A.	„ 12
THE FAMILY OF SIR THOMAS MORE. From the painting by Hans Holbein	„ 21
THE DEATH OF THE REGENT MURRAY. From the drawing by George Cattermole	„ 34
THE INTERIOR OF THE PALACE OF JUSTICE, BRUGES. From a drawing by Thomas Allom . . .	„ 40
ON A LADY PLAYING (LADY WALLSCOURT). From the painting by Sir Thomas Lawrence, P.R.A. . .	„ 44
THE PLAZA REAL AND THE CATHEDRAL, SEVILLE. From a drawing by David Roberts, R.A. . . .	„ 69
SIR WALTER SCOTT AND HIS FAMILY. From the painting by Sir David Wilkie, R.A.	„ 77
THE LADY'S DREAM. From the painting by Thomas Stothard, R.A.	„ 80
LAKE NEMI. From the drawing by J. W. M. Turner, R.A.	„ 96
THE HAPPY ANGLERS. From a drawing by Emile Wattier	„ 115
THE LEANING TOWER OF SARAGOSSA. From a drawing by David Roberts, R.A.	„ 134

THE DUCAL PALACE, VENICE. *From the drawing by Samuel Prout* . . . . . . *To face p.* 139

THE STORM. *From a drawing by Henry Bright* . „ 150

WINDSOR FOREST. *From a drawing by William Leitch and Robert Hills* . . . . . . „ 162

ROUEN—FROM ST. CATHERINE'S HILL. *From the drawing by J. W. M. Turner, R.A.* . . . „ 167

RUSTIC CIVILITY. *From the painting by William Collins, R.A.* . . . . . . „ 171

LETITIA ELIZABETH LANDON (L. E. L.) *From the drawing by Daniel Maclise, R.A.* . . . „ 174

THE RIVER LOIRE AND THE CITY OF TOURS. *From the drawing by J. W. M. Turner, R.A.* . „ 181

THE ENTRY OF EDWARD THE BLACK PRINCE INTO LONDON

By Sir Harris Nicolas

The event which is so admirably illustrated in the accompanying engraving is, perhaps, the most glorious in the annals of England: for history affords few examples of so brilliant a triumph as the victory gained by Edward the Black Prince over King John of France, near Poictiers, on the 19th of September, 1356, or of such important results as it produced.

It is not necessary to detail the circumstances which led to the battle, the amazing disparity of numbers between the two armies, the unrivalled prowess of the Black Prince and his heroic followers, or the engagement itself, for these facts are well known to every reader of English history. The following remarks will, therefore, be confined to the manner in which the French monarch was made prisoner, his treatment by his conqueror, and his reception into London.

Towards the close of the battle, when the success of the English was no longer doubtful, the Prince of Wales demanded of the two French marshals who were brought to him if they knew what had become of their sovereign. On being told that they believed he was either killed or taken, the Prince directed the Earl of Warwick and Sir

Reginald Cobham to ascertain his fate. John, who had performed deeds of personal courage sufficient to establish the fame of the humblest esquire of his army, and had received two wounds in the face, was at that moment in considerable peril. Being driven nearly to the gates of Poictiers, which were closed against him, and Sir Geoffrey de Charny, the bearer of the sacred Oriflamme, who had gallantly fought by his side the whole day, having at last fallen, John became nearly overwhelmed by a crowd of enemies. The honour of capturing the French monarch, and the pecuniary advantage which would arise from it, naturally stimulated the courage of his foes to the uttermost; and his life was, for some time, in imminent danger. But, undismayed by the multitude which pressed upon him, John defended himself and his young son Prince Philip, with incredible valour, long after all hope of rescue was at an end.

The King of France was not, however, destined to surrender to an Englishman. Though two persons, among many competitors, established strong claims to the distinction of having captured him, they were both natives of provinces which had originally been, and have long since again become, integral parts of the French monarchy; and if Froissart be correct, it was one of John's own traitorous subjects who received his sword. The circumstance is best described in that writer's own words :—

'Then there was a great crowd to take the King, and such as knew him cried, "Sir, yield yourself, or else we shall kill you." There was a knight of St. Omer's, retained in pay by the King of England, called Sir Dennis Morbec, who had served the Englishmen five years before, because in his youth he had forfeited the realm of France, for a murder which he committed at St. Omer's. It happened, fortunately for him, that he was next to the King when they were about to take him; he stepped forth into the crowd, and, by the strength of his body and arms, came to the French King, and said in good French—

'"Sir, surrender."

'The King beheld the knight, and said, "To whom shall I yield? Where is my cousin, the Prince of Wales; if I could see him, I would speak with him."

'Dennis answered and said, "Sir, he is not here, but yield to me, and I will conduct you to him."

'"Who are you?" quoth the King.

'"Sir," answered he, "I am Dennis of Morbec, a knight of Artois; but I serve the King of England, because I am banished the realm of France, and have forfeited all my possessions there."

'Then the King gave him his right gauntlet, saying, "I will deliver myself to you."

'There was a great number about the King: for every man compelled him to say he had taken him, so that the King could not proceed, with his young son, the Lord Philip, on account of the crowd.'

Morbec's right to his illustrious prisoner was disputed on the field by no less than ten knights or esquires; and both John and his son were seriously inconvenienced, if not endangered, by the manner in which they enforced their claims. It appears that they had even taken the King and the young Prince from Morbec by force; and his Majesty seems to have been roughly seized by the different competitors, who, in their ardour to support their supposed rights, forgot the respect due to his person. 'The French King,' says Froissart, 'was on foot and in great danger,' when the Earl of Warwick and Sir Reginald Cobham, who had been sent to seek him, arrived, 'for such as were most powerful said, "I have taken him." "Nay," quoth another, "I have taken him." So they contended who should have him. Then the French King, to avoid that danger, said, "Sirs, strive not: lead me and my son courteously to my cousin the Prince, and quarrel not about the taking of me, for I am a lord great enough to make you all rich." The King's words somewhat appeased them: nevertheless, as they went they still continued to make a riot, and challenged the taking of the King.'

Warwick and Cobham hastened to John's protection, and in the Prince of Wales's name imperatively forbad anyone to approach nearer to him, on pain of death. They then dismounted from their horses; and having shown the same marks of deference and respect to the conquered monarch as they would have done to their own sovereign in his 'pride of place,' they conducted him to the Prince of Wales.

The rules of chivalry, which imposed upon a conqueror the duty of treating a vanquished enemy with extreme courtesy, and which happily softened the rigours of war, and had considerable influence on the rude manners of the age, were certain of being faithfully observed by so generous a Prince as Edward. He received John with the reverence and delicacy which a regard for his valour and misfortunes, no less than for his rank, inspired. Seeing him exhausted, the Prince called for wine; and taking it from the bearer, he allowed no one to serve the King but himself. He tendered him the cup upon his knee; and the touching spectacle was presented of a young conqueror, flushed with victory and the heir to a throne, rendering the humblest services to his father's rival within a few moments after he had become his prisoner. Nor was Edward's conduct the mere effect of impulse: for John was treated with equal courtesy and deference during the whole period of his captivity. It was about noon when the King was made prisoner. By the evening all the French nobles who survived the conflict were collected, the more distinguished of whom consisted, besides the King of France and his son Philip, of James of Bourbon, a prince of the blood; the

Archbishop of Sens, and more than forty noblemen of the highest descent and richest domains in the kingdom. A supper was prepared for John and many of his nobility, six of the chief of whom sat with their sovereign at one table. The Prince of Wales appeared as John's attendant, and, when pressed by him to sit by his side, respectfully declined, saying that he was unworthy to sit by so illustrious a Prince, or, in other words, that he had not yet sufficiently distinguished himself in arms. Anxious only to soothe his feelings and reconcile him to his fate, Edward served him at table, in the same manner as he had done his own father after the surrender of Calais; and he is stated by Froissart to have addressed him in the kindest and most flattering terms:—

'Sir,' he said, 'for God s sake make no bad cheer, though your will was not accomplished this day; for, Sir, the King, my father, will certainly bestow on you as much honour and friendship as he can, and will agree with you so reasonably that you shall ever after be friends! and, Sir, I think you ought to rejoice, though the battle be not as you wish, for you have this day gained the high renown of prowess, and have surpassed all others on your side in valour. Sir, I say not this in raillery, for all our party, who saw every man's deeds, agree in this, and give you the palm and chaplet.'

If a modern French writer of the highest reputation has not drawn the incident from his own fertile imagination, rather than from the arid sources of history, the fortitude with which John had hitherto borne his misfortune gave way before the generosity of his conqueror. 'The tears,' says Chateaubriant, 'burst from his eyes and mingled with the marks of blood upon his cheeks.' In their respective stations, all the prisoners received the same attention and kindness from their 'masters'—the term then applied to those who had received the sword of an enemy, without any regard to their relative ranks. Truly indeed has Shakespeare described the Black Prince—

> In war was never lion rag'd more fierce;
> In peace was never gentle lamb more mild.

Nor is it surprising that his conduct should have induced Edward the Third, indulging at once the feelings of a father and of a knight, to declare that his son's behaviour to the French King afforded him even more gratification than the victory itself.

John was conveyed to Bordeaux, where he remained until the following spring, during which time negotiations for peace took place. The news of the victory of Poictiers seems to have reached England early in October, about a fortnight after it was gained; and Geoffrey Hamelyn, a gentleman of the Prince's chamber, who brought the intelligence to England, presented the King with the French monarch's tabard (or tunic) and bacinet, which were probably those he had worn during the conflict. Public thanksgivings were ordered to be offered up throughout the country, and, as might be expected, the event was hailed with joy by all classes. Two remarkable letters from the Black Prince, giving an account of his victory, are preserved, and the modesty and moderation which he showed on every other occasion are therein conspicuous. The first of those letters was written at Bordeaux, on the 22nd of October, and was sent to the Bishop of Worcester by Sir Roger Cottesford, one of his knights, wherein he attributed his success, under Providence, to the bishop's prayers. He enclosed a list of principal prisoners, and said that two thousand four hundred and forty-five of the French men-at-arms had fallen, and that one thousand nine hundred and eighty were taken. The other letter was likewise written at Bordeaux, on the 22nd of October, and was addressed to the mayor, aldermen, and citizens of London, to whom it was conveyed by his chamberlain, Sir Neel Loring, one of the original Knights of the Garter. With the exception of the last passage, the letter, which is a long one, is filled with an account of the proceedings of his army for some time previous to the battle, which event the Prince described in the following brief but striking manner :—

'The battle happened on the day before the eve of Saint Matthew (*i.e.* 19th of September), and, praise be to God! the enemies were discomfited and the King and his son taken; and numerous other eminent persons were taken and killed, as our very dear bachelor, Sir Neel Loring, our chamberlain, the bearer of this, who had the fullest knowledge, will more fully inform you than we can write, to whom we wish you to give entire faith and credence.'

Such, in the fourteenth century, when deeds were considered more eloquent than words, was the laconic despatch of a hero, after defeating an army at least seven times as numerous as his own, and taking a powerful king, his son, and the flower of his nobility prisoners. If modern despatches bear as little resemblance to the Spartan brevity and exemplary modesty of Edward's letters as to the importance of his achievements, the conclusion, wherein the Prince refers to the bearer for further information, is, nevertheless as nearly as possible the style of the present day.

As early as March in the following year, 1357, preparations were made for the arrival of the Prince of Wales and the King of France in England. They were expected to land at Plymouth, and the sheriff of Devonshire was ordered to provide horses for the conveyance of them and their suite.

On the 24th of April the Black Prince and some of the most eminent of his followers, accompanied by the French monarch and his son, sailed from Bordeaux. A ship was assigned for the reception of the King and his retinue; but he was strictly guarded, in consequence of a report that an attempt would be made to rescue him on the passage. Instead of landing at Plymouth, the ship passed that port; and the distinguished passengers disembarked at Sandwich on the 5th of May,[1] at which place they remained two days, to recover from the fatigue of the voyage. On the 8th and 9th they proceeded to Canterbury, where the conqueror and the conquered alike made their offerings to the shrine of Thomas à Becket.

As soon as Edward the Third heard of their arrival, he commanded the Mayor of London to make every preparation for receiving them in the most distinguished manner. From Canterbury the Prince and the French monarch rode to Rochester; on the following day they reached Dartford; and on the next day, Wednesday, the 24th of May, they approached London.

In Southwark, the *cortège* was met by upwards of a thousand of the principal citizens of London, on horseback, headed by the Lord Mayor, and divided into their several companies, which were distinguished by their respective devices and banners, by whom they were conducted into the metropolis. John, who wore his royal robes, was mounted on a large white courser, in token, it is said, of sovereignty; whilst the Prince of Wales, with characteristic humility, rode by his side on a small black horse. Philip, the young French prince, was probably near his father, and must have

[1] Authorities differ respecting the place at which the Prince and the French King landed. They were evidently expected to disembark at Plymouth, which would agree with the length of time that elapsed between their arrival in England, on the 5th of May, and the 24th, when they entered London. There are, however, strong reasons for supposing that they landed at Sandwich, in which case they must have remained nearly ten days at Canterbury. The motive for so long a stay in that city must have been to allow time for preparations for their reception in London.

THE ENTRY OF THE BLACK PRINCE INTO LONDON.

attracted universal sympathy. Having passed over London Bridge, the cavalcade proceeded to Westminster; but their progress was so much impeded by the immense concourse of people, that, though they arrived in London very early in the morning, it was noon before they reached Westminster Hall.

The citizens showed their gratification at the unusual sight of a great monarch, the direst foe of their country, appearing as the captive of the heir of their own sovereign, by erecting triumphal arches, by filling the streets with their richest plate and armour of all kinds, and by decorating their houses with the most valuable tapestry and silks. The clergy, dressed in their full canonical habits, and bearing crosiers, crosses, and censers, formed a conspicuous part of the procession. Martial music, and the acclamations of the populace, were relieved at intervals by hymns of praise and thanksgiving; and the outbursts of national joy were thus subdued by the chastening ceremonies of religion. Youth and age, the citizen, the lawyer, and the churchman, alike forgetful of their vocations, mingled with the throng. Chaplets of flowers were flung from the windows and balconies by the fairest daughters of England; and beauty gave the warriors their best welcome in beaming smiles. But the most interesting object of the day, the 'observed of all observers,' was

The expectancy and rose of the fair state,

the Black Prince. His deportment showed neither exaltation nor pride; and a desire to prevent his illustrious prisoner from feeling mortification and distress seemed only to possess his thoughts. John himself displayed throughout this trying day that dignity and tranquillity which great souls alone are capable of knowing in seasons of adversity. When all the circumstances of this extraordinary assemblage are considered, there is no difficulty in believing the statement of those who were present, that it was the most imposing spectacle ever witnessed in England.

It is this animated scene which the accomplished artist has embodied in the engraving; and when the paucity of materials for such a picture are considered, it is no less remarkable as a work of art than as an effort of imagination.

From the earliest times, the reception of a victorious general, attended by his companions in arms and a long train of prisoners, has always corresponded with the gratitude and admiration of his countrymen. In England, the number of such ovations, on which contemporary chroniclers have, with pardonable vanity, generally delighted to expatiate, are proportionate to the prowess of her soldiers; but, unfortunately, the accounts handed down of the entry of the Black Prince into London, after the battle of Poictiers, are short and unsatisfactory. The historical painter, who may be ambitious of producing a picture worthy of the next great battle gained by an English monarch, will, however, find abundant materials for his purpose, in the full and graphic description of the entry of Henry the Fifth into London, after the battle of Agincourt, by more than one eye-witness of that gorgeous and exhilarating event.

On reaching Westminster Hall, the Prince of Wales conducted John to his father's presence. Edward was seated on his throne, surrounded by many prelates and barons, and vested in all the splendour of majesty.

After the captive monarch had made those reverences which his situation demanded, Edward, touched with the manly dignity with which his adversary supported his misfortune, and animated by his own native generosity, rose eagerly from his throne, and received him with the same marks of respect and esteem as if choice had rendered him his guest, instead of the chances of war his prisoner.

The French King was sumptuously entertained, and apartments were assigned to him in the palace at Westminster until the Savoy could be got ready for his reception. He was afterwards removed to the castles of Hertford, and Somerton, in Lincolnshire, and thence, in March, 1360, to Berkhampstead Castle; and during the whole of John's residence in England, which lasted upwards of three years, he was treated with the attention due to exalted rank and eminent valour in adversity.

THE GARDEN OF BOCCACIO

By S. T. Coleridge

Of late, in one of those most weary hours,
When life seems emptied of all genial powers,
A dreary mood, which he who ne'er has known
May bless his happy lot, I sate alone;
And, from the numbing spell to win relief,
Call'd on the PAST for thought of glee or grief.
In vain! bereft alike of grief and glee,
I sate and cow'r'd o'er my own vacancy!
And as I watched the dull continuous ache,
Which, all else slumb'ring, seem'd alone to wake,
O Friend! long wont to notice yet conceal,
And soothe by silence what words cannot heal,
I but half saw that quiet hand of thine
Place on my desk this exquisite design,
Boccacio's Garden and its faery,
The love, the joyaunce, and the gallantry!
An IDYLL, with Boccacio's spirit warm,
Framed in the silent poesy of form.

Like flocks adown a newly-bathed steep
    Emerging from a mist: or like a stream
Of music soft that not dispels the sleep,
    But casts in happier moulds the slumberer's dream,
Gazed by an idle eye with silent might
The picture stole upon my inward sight.

A tremulous warmth crept gradual o'er my chest,
As though an infant's finger touch'd my breast.
And one by one (I know not whence) were brought
All spirits of power that most had stirr'd my thought
In selfless boyhood, on a new world tost
Of wonder, and in its own fancies lost;
Or charm'd my youth, that, kindled from above,
Loved ere it loved, and sought a form for love;
Or lent a lustre to the earnest scan
Of manhood, musing what and whence is man?
Wild strain of Scalds, that in the sea-worn caves
Rehearsed their war-spell to the winds and waves;
Or fateful hymn of those prophetic maids,
That call'd on Hertha in deep forest glades;
Or minstrel lay, that cheer'd the baron's feast;
Or rhyme of city pomp, of monk and priest,
Judge, mayor, and many a guild in long array,
To high-church pacing on the great saint's day.
And many a verse which to myself I sang,
That woke the tear yet stole away the pang
Of hopes which in lamenting, I renew'd.
And last, a matron now, of sober mien,
Yet radiant still and with no earthly sheen,
Whom as a faery child my childhood woo'd
Even in my dawn of thought—PHILOSOPHY.
Though then unconscious of herself, pardie,
She bore no other name than POESY;
And, like a gift from heaven, in lifeful glee,
That had but newly left a mother's knee,
Prattled and play'd with bird, and flower, and stone
As if with elfin playfellows well known,
And life reveal'd to innocence alone.

Thanks, gentle artist! now I can descry
Thy fair creation with a mastering eye.

And *all* awake! And now in fix'd gaze stand,
Now wander through the Eden of thy hand;
Praise the green arches, on the fountain clear,
See fragment shadows of the crossing deer,
And with that serviceable nymph I stoop
The crystal from its restless pool to scoop.
I see no longer! I myself am there,
Sit on the ground-sward, and the banquet share.
'Tis I, that sweep that lute's love-echoing strings,
And gaze upon the maid who gazing sings:
Or pause and listen to the tinkling bells
From the high tower, and think that there she dwells.
With old Boccacio's soul I stand possest,
And breathe an air like life, that swells my chest.

The brightness of the world, O thou once free,
And always fair, rare land of courtesy!
O Florence! with the Tuscan fields and hills,
And famous Arno fed with all their rills;
Thou brightest star of star-bright Italy!
Rich, ornate, populous, all treasures thine,
The golden corn, the olive, and the vine.
Fair cities, gallant mansions, castles old,
And forests, where beside his leafy hold
The sullen boar hath heard the distant horn,
And whets his tusks against the knarled thorn;
Palladian palace with its storied halls;
Fountains, where LOVE lies listening to their falls;
Gardens, where flings the bridge its airy span,
And Nature makes her happy home with man;
Where many a gorgeous flower is duly fed
With its own rill, on its own spangled bed,
And wreathes the marble urn, or lean its head,
A mimic mourner, that with veil withdrawn
Weeps liquid gems, the presents of the dawn,

Thine all delights, and every muse is thine:
And more than all, the embrace and intertwine
Of all with all in gay and twinkling dance!
Mid gods of Greece and warriors of romance,
See! BOCCACE sits, unfolding on his knees
The new-found roll of old Mæonides;[1]
But from his mantle's fold, and near the heart,
Peers Ovid's HOLY BOOK of Love's sweet Smart!

O all-enjoying and all-blending sage,
Long be it mine to con thy mazy page,
Where, half conceal'd, the eye of fancy views
Fauns, nymphs, and winged saints, all gracious to thy muse!

Still in thy garden let me watch their pranks,
And see in Dian's vest between the ranks
Of the trim vines, some maid that half believes
The *vestal* fires, of which her lover grieves,
With that sly satyr peeping through the leaves!

[1] Boccacio claimed for himself the glory of having first introduced the works of Homer to his countrymen.

THE FAMILY OF SIR THOMAS MORE

The various personages who formed the domestic circle of Sir Thomas More at his house at Chelsea, in 1530, and who are represented in this interesting painting, are now introduced to the reader's particular notice. It is scarcely necessary to observe that the middle-aged person in the centre of the group, under the clock, is

I. Sir Thomas More. He is dressed in dark-coloured robes over a red vest, and has his hands, which are folded together, partly concealed by the sleeves of his gown. Round his neck is a gilt collar of S. S. with a rose suspended to it, and at his feet a small white dog is seated, of the breed called 'Bologna shocks.' Above Sir Thomas is written—'*Thomas Morus, anno* 50.' Of his person, his great-grandson has given the following description, which agrees with the impression conveyed by his portrait. 'He was of mean[1] stature, well proportioned, his complexion tending to phlegmatic; his colour white and pale; his hair neither black nor yellow, but between both; his eyes grey; his countenance amiable and cheerful;' and he adds, 'his voice was neither big nor shrill, but speaking plainly and distinctly; it was not very tunable, though he delighted much in music; his body reasonably healthful, only that towards his latter time, by using much to write, he complained of pains in his breast.' Erasmus tells us that he was in the habit of carrying one shoulder higher than the other, which gave him the appearance of being slightly

[1] Middle.

deformed, and that his hands were larger than agreed with perfect symmetry. Immediately on his right sits

II. SIR JOHN MORE, his father, one of the Judges of the Court of King's Bench, in the robes of which office, of red cloth lined with ermine, he is habited; he wears a black cap on his head, and over him is written—'*Johannes Morus, pater, anno* 76.' Of Sir John's character very little is known; but he must have been possessed of greater merits than are usually ascribed to him, since he was the founder of his family. He was born about 1455; in 1505 was made a serjeant at law; and thirteen years afterwards was raised to the dignity of a Judge of the Court of King's Bench. As he was never promoted, a mean opinion has been formed of his talents; and this impression is inferentially confirmed by two circumstances—the one, that, excepting in revenge for his son's conduct in the House of Commons, he escaped the political dangers with which his times were pregnant, being, perhaps, too insignificant to be cared for; and the other, that, in the epitaph written by Sir Thomas, he is described as being courteous, innocent, meek, merciful, just, and honest: but nothing is said of his wisdom. During the year in which he and his son were contemporary judges, the latter frequently exhibited the most touching examples of filial piety. Though holding the higher office of chancellor, he was accustomed, on passing through Westminster Hall to his own court, to enter the Court of King's Bench; and, if his father had taken his seat, to fall on his knees before him, and reverentially implore his blessing. Sir John More died of a surfeit from having eaten too plentifully of grapes, about November, 1530, having been affectionately attended in his illness by his son, who, on taking his last leave of him, 'with tears, took him about the neck, most lovingly kissed and embraced him, commending his soul devoutly to the merciful hands of Almighty God.'

The figure to the right of Sir John More is

III. ELIZABETH DAUNCEY, and is inscribed—'*Elizabetha Dauncea, Thomæ Mori filia, anno* 21.' She was Sir Thomas's second daughter, and married, when very young, John, son and heir of Sir John Dauncey, and is by far the most beautiful female of the whole group. Mrs. Dauncey is represented as having a fair complexion, with brown eyes and hair, and is putting on her right glove; she is dressed in a black gown, with green sleeves and a gold stomacher, and a kind of chain and her rosary are around her neck; on her head is a black cap, trimmed and tied under her chin with reticulated gold-work; and a white scarf with gold tassels encircles her waist. Under her right arm she holds a book, marked on the outside—'Epistolicæ Senecæ'; and her appearance is altogether extremely prepossessing. Like her sisters, she was well versed in the classical languages, and was the correspondent of the learned Erasmus, who applauded her for the purity of her Latin.

Immediately on her right is

IV. MARGARET CLEMENT, or, as she is described in the picture, '*Uxor Johannis Clement.*' This lady, who was born in 1508, and whose maiden name was Giggs, was distantly related to the More family, and was brought up in Sir Thomas's house. She was educated and loved by him as if she had been one of his own children, and she repaid his kindness with the duty and affection of a daughter. He commences one of his letters in these words: 'Thomas More to his best-beloved children, and to Margaret Giggs, whom he numbereth among his own'; and another, 'Thomas More sendeth greeting to his most dear daughters Margaret, Elizabeth, and Cecily; and to Margaret Giggs, as dear to him as if she were his own.' Her acquirements in Latin and Greek were considerable; and an attachment having been formed between her and the tutor, or, more probably, physician, of the family, Doctor John Clement, she became his wife; on which occasion the antiquary Leland wrote their Epithalamium. When Sir Thomas was conducted to the Tower, after his condemnation, his eldest daughter, this lady, and the wife of his secretary met and embraced him in the tenderest manner. After his death she obtained the shirt in which he suffered, and the hair shirt which, as a kind of penance, he usually wore next his skin, as relics of her martyred benefactor. Mrs. Clements is represented in very plain attire—a black gown, with a white handkerchief over her bosom, and a cap of the same colour; she has a rosary round her neck; to a green girdle, a gold chain and small red bag are suspended; and she holds a book in her left hand, the leaves of which she keeps open with her right.

V. JOHN MORE, the young man to the left of Sir Thomas, was his only son, and is thus described—'*Johannes Morus, Thomæ filius, anno 19.*' His abilities have been much underrated, probably in consequence of his father's witticism, 'that his mother had so long wished for a boy that she had now one who would be a boy as long as he lived'; and some writers have affected to discover indications of weakness in the countenance which Holbein has given him. It is true he did nothing to distinguish himself; but there is ample testimony that, though he was not perhaps possessed of his father's or even of his sisters' talents, he was by no means destitute of intellectual powers. Sir Thomas, in one of his letters, particularly commends the purity of his Latin, and says he had written to him elegantly and pleasantly, returning jest for jest. Grynœus has celebrated his proficiency in Greek, and both he and Erasmus dedicated one of their works to him. He evinced his duty and affection for his father by throwing himself at his feet and embracing him on his way to the Tower after his trial; and he possessed sufficient strength of character to deny the king's supremacy after Sir Thomas's execution, in consequence of which he remained for some time a prisoner under sentence of death. On being released he is presumed to have retired to his wife's estate in Yorkshire, his paternal property having been confiscated, and died in 1547. At a very early age he married,

VI. ANNE CRESACRE, the pretty-looking girl who stands at a little distance behind, in the space between Sir Thomas and Sir John, dressed in black, over whom is written—'*Anna Cresacre, Johannis Mori sponsa, anno* 15.' She was the daughter and heiress of Edward Cresacre, of Barnborough, in Yorkshire, Esq., the last male representative of an ancient family. Though called fifteen in the picture, she must have been much nearer eighteen, as she was one year old at her father's decease in 1512. Her grandson says she was married by mistake, or, as he expresses it, 'upon error for another body's lands;' for Sir Thomas, proceeding on the feudal plan, intended to purchase the marriage of a coheiress who held one moiety of his estate, but from some accident the treaty was concluded for Anne Cresacre, who accordingly became his son's wife. She survived her husband many years, and fulfilled the duties of her station very creditably, having educated her numerous family of five sons and one daughter, and recovered their hereditary lands in Herefordshire. In June, 1559, she married her second husband, George West, Esq., and in the same year her only daughter married John West, her husband's son by his first wife. She again became a widow in 1572, and died at Barnborough on the 2nd of December, 1577, in her sixty-sixth year.

The three ladies in the corner are

In the foreground, with a clasped book in her lap, and looking to the top, CECILY HERON, on the bottom of whose gown is written —'*Cæcilia Herona, Thomæ filia, anno*

THE FAMILY OF SIR THOMAS MORE.

By Hans Holbein.

20.' She was Sir Thomas's third and youngest daughter, and married when very young Giles Heron, of Shackelwel, in Middlesex, Esq., son of Sir John Heron, Master of the Jewel House, by whom she had a son, Thomas, who died issueless. Her literary acquirements equalled those of her sisters, and received the same commendations. Like those of the other females, her dress is black velvet or cloth, with red sleeves and a gold stomacher; and, besides her rosary, she has an ornament suspended by a black riband from her neck.

Next to her sits the celebrated

MARGARET ROPER, who is described on her gown as— '*Margareta Ropera, Thomæ Mori filia, anno 22.*' She was Sir Thomas More's eldest and favourite daughter, and resembled him more nearly than the rest of his children in the depth and acuteness of her understanding. Of this eminent woman much is said in the various memoirs of her father; but the space to which this sketch of her must be confined will only allow of the most striking facts being noticed. Sir Thomas was so devoted to her that, during a dangerous illness with which she was visited, he resolved if she had died to withdraw himself wholly from the world; and her recovery is imputed to the efficacy of his prayers. She was the dispenser of her father's secret charities, and to her alone he entrusted the knowledge of the severe religious austerities to which he subjected himself—his hair shirt and his repeated scourgings. In some of these self-inflicted penances she imitated her parent: 'She had her shirts and girdles of hair,' says Bishop Fisher in one of his sermons, 'which, when she was in health, every week she failed not certain days to wear, sometime the one, sometime the other, that full often her skin, as I heard say, was pierced therewith.' Although Mrs. Roper's veneration for her father scarcely knew any limits, it is remarkable that she not only took the obnoxious oath, with the qualification, however, 'as far as it would stand with the law of God,' but used every argument to induce him to follow her example. A most affecting scene took place between them on his return to the Tower after his condemnation, which it would be a want of judgment to describe in any other words than those of her husband: 'When Sir Thomas More came from Westminster to the Tower-ward again, his daughter, my wife, desirous to see her father, whom she thought she should never see in this world after, and also to have his final blessing, gave attendance about the Tower Wharf, where she knew he should pass by before he could enter into the Tower. There tarrying his coming, as soon as she saw him, after his blessing upon her knees reverently received, she, hasting towards him, without consideration or care of herself, pressing in amongst the midst of the throng and company of the guard, that with halberds and bills went round about him, hastily ran to him, and there openly, in sight of them all, embraced him, and took him about the neck and kissed him; who, well liking her most natural and dear daughterly affection towards him, gave her his fatherly blessing, and many godly words of comfort besides. From whom, after she was departed, she, not satisfied with the former sight of her dear father, and like one that had forgotten herself, being all ravished with the entire love of her dear father, having respect neither to himself nor to the press of people and multitude that were there about him, suddenly turned back again, ran to him as before, took him about the neck, and divers times kissed him most lovingly; and at last, with a full and heavy heart, was fain to depart from him: the beholding whereof was to many of them that were present thereat so lamentable that it made them for very sorrow thereof to weep and mourn.'

The morning before he suffered Sir Thomas privately sent her his hair shirt and scourge, together with the following letter, written with a piece of charcoal in a copy of one of his works. ' It is particularly deserving of insertion, from the allusions which it contains to most of the persons who have been mentioned in this memoir, and must be read with the deepest interest.

'Our Lord bless you, good daughter, and your good husband, and your little boy, and all yours, and all my children, and all my god-children, and all our friends. Recommend me, when ye may, to my good daughter Cecily, whom I beseech our good Lord to comfort ; and I send her my blessing, and to all her children, and pray her to pray for me. I send her an handkerchief, and God comfort my good son, her husband. My good daughter Daunce hath the picture in parchment that you delivered me from my Lady Coniers : her name is on the back side. Show her that I heartily pray her that you may send it in my name, to her again, for a token from me to pray for me. I like special well Dorothy Colly ; I pray you be good unto her. I would wit whether this be she that you wrote me of ; if not, yet I pray you be good to the other as you may, in her affliction, and to my daughter Joan Aleyn, too.[1] Give her, I pray you, some kind answer, for she sued hither to me this day to pray you be good to her. I cumber you, good Margaret, much, but I would be sorry if it should be any longer than to-morrow, for it is St. Thomas' even, and the utas of Saint Peter ; and therefore to-morrow long I to go to God : it were a day very meet and convenient for me.[2] I never liked your manners towards me better than when you kissed me last, for I love when daughterly love and dear charity hath no leisure to look to worldly courtesy. Farewell, my dear child, and pray for me, and I shall for

---

[1] A servant of Mrs. Roper, perhaps his god-daughter, or, like Margaret Clement, on whom he bestows the same appellation, one of his *protégées*.

[2] St. Thomas was probably his tutelar saint.

you, and all your friends, that we may merrily meet in heaven. I thank you for your great cost. I send now to my good daughter Clement her algorisme stone, and I send her and my godson, and all hers, God's blessing and mine. I pray you at time convenient recommend me to my good son John More. I liked well his natural fashion.[1] Our Lord bless him and his good wife, my loving daughter, to whom I pray him to be good, as he hath great cause ; and that if the land of mine come to his hand, he break not my will concerning his sister Daunce. And our Lord bless Thomas and Austen,[2] and all that they shall have.'

It was one of his last requests to Henry that his daughter Margaret might attend his funeral. In defiance of the danger which attended the act, she bought the head of her ill-fated parent, when it was about to be thrown into the Thames, after having been affixed to London Bridge ; and on being questioned by the Privy Council about her conduct, she boldly replied that she had done so that 'it might not become food for fishes.' She survived Sir Thomas nine years, and died, aged 36, in 1544, and was buried in the church of St. Dunstan, at Canterbury, the box containing her father's head being placed on her coffin. By her husband, who lived a widower thirty-three years, and died in January, 1577, aged eighty-two, she had issue two sons and three daughters, one of the latter of whom is noticed by Mr. Ballard in his memoirs of celebrated women. The present representative of Mrs. Roper is Charles Winn, of Nostell Priory, in Yorkshire, Esq., the possessor of Holbein's painting.[3] She sent Erasmus a copy of it, which he acknowledged in a letter to her, expressive of the delight which the present afforded him, wherein a family so highly esteemed were exactly pourtrayed ; adding that, though he knew each of the figures the instant he saw them, yet was

---

[1] Alluding to their conduct on meeting him after his condemnation.
[2] His son's children.   [3] In 1830.

he more particularly pleased with her portrait, which recalled to his mind all the excellent qualities he had so long admired in her. The painting [1] sent to Erasmus, which was likewise by Holbein, is carefully preserved in the town hall of Basel. Mrs. Roper's extraordinary erudition excited the admiration of the most learned of her contemporaries; and her father, on more than one occasion, repeats with a parent's pride the compliments which had been paid to her compositions. She is painted in a dress very similar to her sister's; but the sleeves are ornamented with gold, and her stomacher, which is red, has a jewel in the upper part. A book is open in her lap, on which is written—'L. An. Senecæ—Œdipus,' as a running title; and the page commences with 'Fata si liceat mihi fingere arbitrio meo, temperem zephyro levi.'

The old lady behind Mrs. Roper, near the monkey, holding a book before her, is

ALICE LADY MORE, over whom is written—'*Alicia, uxor Thomæ Mori, anno 57.*' She was the second wife of Sir Thomas More, and was the daughter and heiress, or co-heiress, of —— Arderne, and widow of John Middleton, by whom she had a daughter, Alice, to whom her stepfather behaved with a tenderness which she gratefully acknowledged during his misfortunes: she married first Thomas Eldrington, Esq., who died at Chelsea, in September, 1523; and, secondly, Sir Giles Allington, Knight, and was buried at Horsheath, in Cambridgeshire, on the 26th of September, 1563. Lady More was seven years older than her husband: she was neither rich nor handsome; and, from what his great-grandson says of her, it would seem that Sir Thomas was tricked into the alliance, thus proving that his boasted talents were but an unequal match for

> That low cunning which in fools supplies,
> And amply, too, the place of being wise.

---

[1] It is an outline only.

All which is known of her justifies our considering that she was both ignorant and vulgar—a coarse weed in the parterre into which it was her singular fortune to be transplanted. A letter from her to Secretary Cromwell exhibits a most affecting picture of the distress to which Sir Thomas's imprisonment had reduced his family, and excites our warmest sympathy for his misfortunes. Her motive for writing is, she says, to inform him 'of my great and extreme necessity, which, over and besides the charge of mine own house, do pay weekly fifteen shillings for the board wages of my poor husband and his servant, for the maintaining whereof I have been compelled, of very necessity, to sell part of mine apparel, for lack of other substance to make money of'; and she entreated to be allowed to appear before the Privy Council.

The stout man next to John More, and immediately behind Mrs. Heron, standing with his face *affronté*, is

HENRY PATTISON—'*Henricus Pattison, Thomæ servus*' —one of the degraded creatures whom, by the title of 'Fool, it was then the fashion to keep in most families of distinction. He is represented, in a dress of three colours, the undermost being red, the next, which is a sort of jacket, is green, and over all he wears a kind of yellow frock. In his round black cap are two roses, the one white, and the other red; on the left side is a small shield charged, with a red cross, and near it what seems to be a jewel. Round his neck a gold cross, or, more likely, a whistle, is suspended, and the thumb of his left hand seems to rest in his girdle. Pattison appears to have been a stout, healthy man, about forty, with a florid complexion, blue eyes, and a countenance which does not betray any want of intellect.

Of the two remaining figures only one can be identified, for the name of the person habited in a green gown, standing at a window in another room, holding a black-letter volume in his hands, is not known. The man enter-

ing the door, dressed in a tawny-coloured gown, holding in
his left hand a roll of parchment, with seals attached, and
in his right what seems to be a large pair of spectacles, is
JOHN HARRIS, or, as the writing over his head describes
him, '*Johannes Heresius, Thomæ Mori famul'*, *anno* 27,'
who was Sir Thomas More's secretary, and a most favoured
servant. He married Dorothy Colly, who has been already
mentioned ; but an anecdote relating to her, which the
superstition of Cresacre More makes him consider a miracle,
cannot be inserted in a more appropriate place. Mrs.
Roper, having distributed all her money to the poor to say
masses for her father's soul, forgot to buy a sheet to wrap
his body in ; and neither she, Mrs. Clement, nor Mrs.
Harris, united, possessed sufficient to purchase one. The
latter, notwithstanding, went into a draper's shop, and
having agreed on the price, pretended to seek for her purse,
with the intention of afterwards asking them to trust her,
when, to her astonishment, she found the exact sum which
she required, though she knew positively there was not a
farthing in it when she entered the shop. Harris died at
Neumarch, in Germany, and is buried there, in the same
grave with his son-in-law, John Fowler, a native of Bristol,
who settled at Antwerp as a printer.

The bipeds in the painting having been described, the
monkey and dogs, which are introduced in it, require a
slight notice. Sir Thomas More's love of natural history
accounts for the appearance of the former, and one of the
dogs may be supposed, from the date of the picture being
nearly that of the year in which Sir Thomas held the great
seal, to be the hero of the following story, which is told by
Cresacre More.

'It happened on a time that a beggar-woman's little
dog, which she had lost, was presented for a jewel to my
Lady More, and she had kept it some se'nnight very carefully ; but at last the beggar had notice where her dog was,

and presently she came to complain to Sir Thomas, as he was sitting in his hall, that his lady withheld her dog from her; presently my lady was sent for, and the dog brought with her; which Sir Thomas taking in his hands, caused his wife, because she was the worthier person, to stand at the upper end of the hall and the beggar at the lower end, and, saying that he sat there to do everyone justice, he bade each of them call the dog, which when they did, the dog went presently to the beggar, forsaking my lady. When he saw this he bade my lady be contented, for it was none of hers; yet, she repining at the sentence of my lord chancellor, agreed with the beggar, and gave her a piece of gold, which would well have bought three dogs, and so all parties were agreed, every one smiling to see his manner of inquiring out the truth.'

The room in which the group are represented is presumed to have been in Sir Thomas's house at Chelsea, the furniture of which is strongly indicative of the taste and pursuits of the family. At the upper end stands a chamber organ, on a cupboard, with a curtain drawn before it. The cupboard is covered with a carpet-cloth of tapestry, on each end of which is placed a flower-pot filled with various flowers; and in the centre a lute, a base-viol, a ewer with a white cloth folded over it; and three books, one of which is *Boetius de Consolatione Philosophiæ*, a favourite author of the family, who is thus mentioned in one of Sir Thomas More's letters to Mrs. Roper:—' I admonish you also to think of this holy fast of Lent, and let that excellent and pious song of Boethius sound in your ears.' Behind Lady More, in a large arched window, stands another flower-pot and a couple of oranges beside it, whilst the representation of the apartment itself, with the clock, which is still preserved, chairs, &c., affords a correct idea of the sitting-rooms of persons of consequence in the early part of the sixteenth century.

THE DEATH OF THE REGENT MURRAY

BY SIR WALTER SCOTT

> Sternly he spoke—'Tis sweet to hear
> In good green wood the bugle blown;
> But sweeter to Revenge's ear,
> To hear a tyrant's dying groan.

AN event now occurred which startled the regent like a thunderbolt. Mary, although a captive in the hands of her enemies, and in the midst of a lonely lake, was yet formidable in her arms of grace and beauty, in her queenly majesty, and her woman's tears. Young Douglas of Lochleven, at once pitying her misfortunes and smitten with her charms, contrived their escape. On a dark night, and at the witching hour, they left the island.

The sentinel, whose slumbering had withstood the whispering, was alarmed by the dash of oars. His challenge was instantly heard. 'A boat—a boat! Bring to, or I shoot!' And as they continued to ply their oars, he called aloud, 'Treason! treason!' rang the alarm-bell of the castle, and discharged his harquebuss at the boat. The ladies crowded on each other like startled wild-fowl, at the flash and report of the piece, while the men urged the rowers to the utmost speed. They heard more than one ball whiz along the surface of the lake, at no great distance from their little bark; and from the lights, which glanced like meteors from window to window, it was evident that the whole castle were alarmed and their flight discovered.

Mary, however, effected her escape, and soon found herself once more at the head of an army. But even now the regent did not lose his presence of mind ; but, by his promptitude and vigour, no less than by the wisdom of his plans, proved himself to belong to that class of men who should be termed the parents rather than the sons of destiny. He attacked and routed the enemy at Langside, with a far inferior force, and compelled the queen to the fatal step of flying for refuge into the tigress's den, whence she was never to escape alive. The victory should be termed 'glorious' (if the word were not so vilely prostituted as to be worth nothing), for it was bought with the loss of only three hundred lives ; and even six of the prisoners, whom he had selected for execution, were spared, when on the scaffold, at the intercession of John Knox.

Among the six prisoners there was one man whose life it proved the keenest, yet probably unconscious, cruelty to spare. This was Bothwellhaugh, a gentleman of the clan of Hamilton, and a blood relation of its chief, the Earl of Arran (Duke of Chatelherault in France), the first peer of the realm. He had married the heiress of Woodhouselee, and resided with her in her own ancestral home in the lovely vale of Esk, and where she had just given birth to a child. At this moment the tocsin sounded throughout Scotland ; the queen had escaped from Lochleven ; and the loyal Hamilton, tearing himself away from his new-born hope and his young wife, ran to join the muster of his clan.

The result of the struggle is known. Mary stood on a hill to look on at the battle which was to decide her fate ; and the Hamiltons in the van, led on by Lord Claud Hamilton, knowing that they fought under the eye of 'the most unhappy of queens, the most lovely of women,' left their ground in a burst of enthusiasm, and rushed on to the encounter. The space between them and the enemy was considerable, and their force was almost spent before they came to close quarters. When at length the spears of the two opposing lines were locked together like the arms of lovers, and the tug of battle commenced, a continuous fire of musketry opened upon one of their flanks, while on their other they were attacked by the élite of the regent's troops. The main body of Mary's adherents behind, disheartened by a spectacle for which they were unprepared, or controlled by the destiny of the fated queen, remained stupefied; and the Hamiltons, unsupported, or rather sacrificed, gave way, and the battle became a flight.[1]

When Bothwellhaugh, a dishonoured soldier and a condemned criminal, ascended the scaffold soon after, it may be conceived with what feelings he turned his eyes towards the south, and saw in imagination his 'pallid rose' drooping feebly yet fondly over his little bud. When delivered from death—he scarcely understood why or how—it may be conceived how eagerly he spurred his steed towards the lonely valley of the Esk.

To describe the scene which met his view, and the tale which knelled in his ear, without a creeping of the flesh, a curdling of the blood, and a sickening of the heart, is impossible. His estate of Woodhouselee had been given away to a favourite of the regent; and this man, Sir James Ballenden, eager to enter upon his new possession, had seized the house at night and turned its mistress and her infant out into the open fields. The young mother had but lately risen from the bed of her confinement; she was undressed; the night was bitterly cold. The result is told to this day in the superstitions of the peasants of the Esk, who see a lady thinly clad in white, with an infant in her arms, flitting wildly around the spot where the mansion stood. A

---

[1] Melville says that the vanguard was composed chiefly of commoners of the neighbouring barony of Renfrew.

frenzied scream sometimes thickens their blood with horror, as the phantom sinks among the ruins.

Bothwellhaugh turned back from Woodhouselee.

Sir James Ballenden, who held a high and honourable office in the law, would have been a fair mark for vengeance under any ordinary circumstances. But the wrongs of the Hamilton were not such as could be weighed in the common balance of blood. Something must be done—he knew not what. Something that would shake the very realm to its centre. Something that would be heard by every ear in Scotland, as distinctly as the scream of the lady of Woodhouselee had thrilled along the Esk. Sir James Ballenden was but an agent, a servant—a pitiful, dastardly hound, who only worried at the command or under the protection of his master. That master was the true offender. The blood of the first man in the country would be a fitting libation. Hamilton of Bothwellhaugh determined to slay the regent of Scotland.

He dogged his steps for some time like fate. He followed him to the Borders, and when the regent had dismissed his army, at a motion of Elizabeth's royal finger, returned upon his traces to Edinburgh. He was with him in York and London, when Murray went crouching to the footstool of the English queen, to prefer a charge of murder against his sister; in Perth, in Glasgow, in Stirling, he hovered around him, like a bird of prey circling above its quarry, and only awaiting an opportunity to strike.

The regent, in the meantime, held on his way, successful alike in policy and war. When about to pass through Linlithgow, on his way from Stirling to Edinburgh, a warning reached him. It came from John Knox, and the first-named place was mentioned as the spot of danger. There was nothing preternatural in the foresight of the Scottish apostle; for the frightful wrongs of Bothwellhaugh were already well known, and Linlithgow, besides being favourable to the cause of the queen, was a seat of the Archbishop of St. Andrews, who had there a house,[1] which was more particularly pointed out to the regent as the place to be avoided.

Constitutionally brave, and steeled yet more against the sense of danger by a long course of daring and success, James Stewart smiled scornfully at the warning. Was *his* wonderful destiny in the hands of the petty laird of Bothwellhaugh? Was the blood of a line of Scottish kings to sink in the ground at the command of a vassal of Hamilton? In vain had the Earl of Huntly beset his path, as if he had been stalking a deer; in vain had Bothwell—in vain had Darnley, raised the dagger against his breast; in vain, but a few months ago, had a hedge of Northumberland and Westmoreland spears risen up to prevent his return to Scotland alive. All were in vain. Secure alike from war and treachery, he bore a charmed life; and when his gallant steed swerved at the sight and cheers of the tumultuous crowd, as they commenced their march through Linlithgow, the regent probably addressed him inwardly with the Roman's encouragement—'Quid timeas? Cæsarem vehis et fortunam Cæsaris!'

At this moment, however, the warning was repeated still more emphatically—perhaps for no better reason than that they were now approaching the house of the Archbishop of Saint Andrews; the alarm spread among the friends who encircled him, and murmurs arose that it was madness to expose a life so precious to them, and to the kingdom, to any unnecessary risk. The regent himself began to think that his danger was something more than imaginary; and, at length, turning his horse, he gave orders to the cortège to face about, resolving to quit Linlithgow by the same gate by which he had entered, and make a circuit round the town.

The house which had excited their fears, and which they

[1] The archbishop was the natural brother of the Duke of Chatelherault (the chief of the Hamiltons) and uncle to Bothwellhaugh.

had thus left behind, formed part of the line of buildings; and a sort of gallery, or apartment, projecting from the walls, overlooked the street. In this gallery stood the Revenger, a brass carabine of peculiar construction, the barrel being rifled, raised to his eye, and a lighted match grasped between his fingers. The floor was carpeted with a feather-bed, that no sound might be heard from his footsteps, and the wall behind was hung with black cloth, that his shadow might not be observed by the passers-by. A fleet horse stood saddled and bridled at the back door, the front entrance was strongly barricaded, and the *closes*, or covered courts, in the neighbourhood, leading to the rear of the houses, were stuffed with furze. And so stood Bothwellhaugh, his eye fixed grimly on the visy of his piece; his lips as hard as stone, yet half open with expectation; and impatience, mingled with iron resolve, scowling on his brow.

When the regent reached the gate of the town he found the crowd of citizens, thus thrust back, struggling with a tide of population, rushing in with equal force, from the neighbouring country, to see the show. The way was for the moment impassable; and Murray, chafing with impatience, scorned to wait till it was cleared. Changing his determination as suddenly and as unconsciously as before, he turned his horse again, and passed on his allotted path.

It may be that, on finding himself again pursuing the same track against which he had been warned, and which he had but a few minutes before determined to shun, some unusual sensation passed across his heart. It may be that his thoughts were carried at that moment, by association, to the other epochs of his wonderful story. Perhaps the heart-broken moan of his queen and sister rose upon his ear; perhaps the frenzied scream of the lady of Woodhouselee pierced through his brain. These are the speculations of poetry. We only know that the regent, determining to defy and baffle the danger which it seemed he

Woodburt-Gravure.

could not shun, called to his followers to dash hastily past the archbishop's house, and thus frustrate the scheme, if any such existed, of his lurking enemy.

> Dark Morton, girt with many a spear,
>   Murder's foul minion, led the van;
> And clash'd their broadswords, in the rear,
>   The wild Macfarlan's plaided clan.
>
> Glencairn, and stout Parkhead, were nigh,
>   Obsequious at their regent's rein,
> And haggard Lindsay's iron eye,
>   That saw fair Mary weep in vain.

But the regent could not dash over the bodies of his countrymen, and would not if he had been able. The crowd before was as dense as the crowd behind; every dwelling, every close continued to pour its quota into the flood. They were near the house of the archbishop, and perhaps the very circumstance retarded their progress, from the eagerness of the vassals to crowd round their master at the dangerous spot, and, if need was, to die with him, or for him. The order of the line was broken; the chief was encircled by devoted friends; and only now and then the wave of his proud plumes could be discerned from the gallery among the crowd of heads. They were opposite the house. The window was open, but the gallery empty; for there was no footstep on the floor, no shadow on the wall. They did not see the glare of the tiger-eye of Bothwellhaugh—the damp of deadly hate standing on his brow—the hand which clutched the carabine trembling with impatience. Another moment and the regent is safe. It came not. A shot was heard above the cheers of the crowd; and he fell mortally wounded from his horse.[1]

---

[1] The fire-lock of the carabine in the engraving involves an anachronism, for which Mr. Cattermole is not to blame. The piece is preserved at Hamilton Palace; but somebody, from a singular species of taste, has thought proper to replace the original matchlock with the modern invention.

To mark the fate of his victim; to fly to the rear of the building; to bound upon his steed, were but the occupations of an instant. The Revenger gained the open country unmolested: for to force an entrance into the house was a work of time; and he fled, at full speed, towards Hamilton, the capital of his clan. But not alone. Leaving their comrades to force an entrance as they might, some readyminded vassals of the regent had darted away, almost at the moment of the deed, to intercept him. Owing to more accurate knowledge of the neighbourhood of the town, he had the start; but now, serving as a guide himself, the whole party, pursuers and pursued, scoured over the heath together.

Bothwellhaugh was hardly a spear's-throw in advance; but his horse, which had been the gift of Lord John Hamilton, was all muscle and mettle. Onward the noble brute bounded—straight as an arrow—over field and moss and dyke and burn. When his strength began to fail whip and spur were applied, till his sides welled blood and sweat at the same time. But even the rowels at length failed in their effect, and the sense of pain became dead in the wide wound they had formed. The pursuers were close upon his heels. At every leap he had taken, however mad and desperate, they had come thundering after; and he now distinctly heard the groan-like panting of their steeds and the sobs with which the riders caught breath as they flew.

A stream was in front, broad, deep, and sluggish, winding through a morass. There was no purchase in the soft ground for the animal's heels, even if in full vigour for the leap; but, spent as he was, and callous even to the spur, what hope remained? Bothwellhaugh, however, still held on his course. As he neared the water he tried the rowels again to the very hilt—without effect. A hoarse cheer arose from the pursuers behind. He then suddenly drew his dagger, as he had gained the brink, struck it deep into his horse's haunch, and the affrighted animal sprang madly over the gulf.

He was now safe, and arrived speedily at Hamilton, where he was received in triumph by his friends and clan. After having remained there for some time, Bothwellhaugh passed over into France, and offered his services to the Guises, the kinsmen of the Queen of Scots. By them he was treated with much distinction; and even a circumstance which he felt as a bitter insult was probably intended as the very reverse. When it was the question among them to murder the famous Coligny, the leader of the Protestant party, overtures were made to the Scottish assassin, with the view of engaging him to strike the blow. Bothwellhaugh spurned at the proposal with scorn and indignation. 'The admiral,' he said, 'was no personal enemy of his. A man of honour was entitled to avenge his own just quarrels, but would cease to be so if he committed murder for another.'

I may add that the Archbishop of St. Andrews, two months afterwards, fell into the hands of his enemies at the capture of Dumbarton Castle, and was hanged without ceremony; and that the heir of the Regent Murray was murdered in the prime of his youth by the Earl of Huntly.

THE PALACE OF JUSTICE, BRUGES

By Thomas Roscoe

The Palace of Justice, erected in 1722, on the east side of the town—formerly Palais du Franc de Bruges (the Liberty), forming an independent district, was given up by Philip the Good to the magistracy of the Franc de Bruges. It presents nothing very remarkable in the façade, but in the work of Sanderus, where you see a full representation of the ancient edifice, it is different. As represented also in the accompanying view it serves to convey, both in point of character and costume, a perfect and lively idea of the scene it once exhibited, in the palmier days of Flemish law and justice. It is the interior which deserves the study of the antiquary; and among other objects of art he will remark, in one of the halls, the grand chimney-piece, so admirably sculptured in wood as to astonish the connoisseurs of every country. From a date upon one of the sides it appears that this elaborate work was executed in the year 1529. The genii and the bas-reliefs which adorn the frieze are all in white marble; and represent with equal care the history of Susannah. The stately figure in the centre is the Emperor Charles V.; on his left are seen the statues of Maximilian, and of Mary of Burgundy; on the right, those of Charles the Bold, and Margaret of England, his third wife. Upon the two sides, above these figures, are given the emblems and coats of arms of Spain, Bur-

PALACE OF JUSTICE. BRUGES.

gundy, Brabant, and Flanders, all finished with an exquisite degree of art.[1]

Here, too, besides a series of portraits of Spanish sovereigns, is preserved a large painting by Van Oost, the son, chiefly distinguished for the exquisite truth of the fleshes and the vivacity of the colouring. In the hall, now appropriated to the use of the police, is another picture by J. Van Oost, the father, which represents a criminal, and in which it is said are also represented the portraits of the judges who lived at the period of the trial. The background gives a view of the hall to which we have alluded, and it may be observed that it has very little changed its appearance. Over the chimney itself is seen a fine landscape, by Joseph de Momper, with figures and animals by Breughel de Velours, in that peculiarly happy style which then came so much into vogue.

In the chamber where the judges assemble previous to holding their sessions there is a splendid view of the town as it appeared at that period, with its now antique aspect and picturesque character fresh upon it. It is interesting to contrast the past with the present, and observe the numerous changes and dilapidations which have rendered the latter a comparatively grand ruin—the sad, but picturesque cemetery of its own fortunes. Over the chimney of the Hall of the Tribunal appears an allegorical picture of some merit, which represents Philip the Good seated on a throne, in the act of granting a charter, bearing the date of 1435; and farther on, in the chamber of advocates, we noticed a painting of the Decapitation of St. John, tolerably well executed, and other specimens, chiefly copies of older masters by Gaeremyn and Suvée, besides some portraits of Spanish sovereigns, and two or three landscapes.

---

[1] This grand piece of wood-carving was designed and probably executed by Lancelot Blondeel and Guyot de Beaugrant. A cast of the whole chimney-piece may be seen in the South Kensington Museum.

In this palace are also found deposited the provincial archives, among which are contained charters, which may be traced back to the twelfth century, and they are almost innumerable.

No amateur who delights in viewing selected specimens of the highest character, will fail to visit M. Chantrell's collection of sketches by Rubens, and some admirable prints by the early masters. We found that of M. Steinmetz equally rich in paintings and in prints, in the German, Dutch, and Italian schools. Add to these the several collections of Messrs. Vanden-Bussche, Puyenbeke, and Baron de Marenzi, which exhibit some rare and excellent specimens of the arts in their different stages, which would agreeably occupy not only hours, but days, and even weeks, in the opinion of genuine connoisseurs and all who have the happiness to possess a taste for them. 'You will now be enabled,' said the count, ' to form some idea of old Flemish art, and to acquit Lanzi of any desire to depreciate its excellence. Nay, I trust to make a convert of you, to all my Flemish doctrines, before you join your friends at Liége. We will go together ; at every step you will see something worth your notice, and you will oblige me,' he added, 'for I will show you our *schools* of painting, as we are not singular, " our name is legion " ; from fine old Van Eyck, to my studious friend and true scholar De Keyser. There is also Geefs, too, and his studio, full of classic models—I mean his own—there is Verbeckhoeven, the very Landseer of Belgium, and our provinces have each their painters and their pupils, who, if not as successful as they deserve, have less to blame themselves, their genius, or their talents, than the adverse spirit of their age. It is the same with your historical painters : it is only when your artists reflect your own likeness, and something better, perhaps, that they are really popular with you. I think that of the two, we are the more just ; look at your John Martin, how he was received here; his Belgian reputation is perhaps worth more than his English, though that deservedly stands high. But the stream of emigration in art, as in everything else, is from you and towards your colonies, or us younger resuscitated states. And this is honourable for you; Britain is the foster-mother of many lands, of the peaceful arts, and of a certain degree of freedom, not well defined indeed, but good as compared with the absolutism so oppressive in other parts. She is the arbitress of Europe, and the hope of the world.'

I made the count a profound obeisance, when he added, with a malicious smile: 'but you are without a pictorial history; you must still visit Italy and Flanders if you wish to have it; Bruges, Brussels, and Antwerp abound with native masters, who yield to none. If we have no Michael Angelo, and no Raphael, we need not shrink from a comparison with any other names. Fix your eye steadily a few minutes on our old Van Eycks, study our Memling, our Rubens, and he who combined the merits of all, the universal Van Dyck, and mark how boldly they confront the Giottos, the disciples of Perugino, Titian himself, Paul Veronese, Guido, and the Carracci. While they have nothing to confound them even with Rembrandt, much less the second-rate Dutch, with the Ostades or the Brouwers. See our Van Dyck at Ghent, and some of those noble portraits, carrying us back to the moral grandeur, the stern heroic devotion of a different age, which impress a glory on his saints, and radiate from the noble heads which give life to the walls of the palace of the Prince of Brussels. Compared with these, what are the Dutch but models of their own *bambocciati*? Our Flemish painters, inspired by the example of Rubens and Van Dyck, travelled; were men of the world, and carried art and civilisation into other lands. But the Dutch masters, still more than the French and English, almost invariably remained at home.' I ventured to remind the young enthusiast of his country's art of not a few French, English, and even Dutch masters who had travelled, and instanced the name of Wander—no inappropriate one for the occasion. 'They are examples, I grant,' was the ingenious reply, 'but only to prove the truth of my general observation; and what was the use of travel, when they all returned home, more English, French, and Dutch, and yet more *bambocciati*, if I may so say, than when they left it. It was different with the Flemish school; who was the master of Guido and first put him into the right path, but our Calvaert, *il Fiamingo* of Italy? Our Luigi Pozzo was the best landscape painter of his day; and Brill was better known in Venice and over all Italy than many great Italians themselves. Our David Teniers is in himself a host! and our Crayer and Jordaens, both masters in their several lines.' 'Still,' I observed, 'we ought not to forget there have lived such men as Rembrandt, Paul Potter, and Gerard Dou.'

'I know and appreciate them,' was the count's reply; 'I do not deny that they possessed positive merit, but of a different, and, I believe, inferior kind. In our Flemish school, as in those of Italy, however, there is a splendour and a charm peculiar to them, and in both, I conceive, national and original. And of both we may aver with the felicitous enthusiasm of La Fontaine, the happy poet of painting, in words which express the spirit of Flemish art—

> A de simples couleurs cet art plein de magie
> Sait donner du relief, de l'âme et de la vie.
> Ce n'est rien qu'une toile, et l'on croit voir un corps.
> Il évoque à son gré les vivants et les morts;
> Il transporte les yeux aux confins de la terre;
> Il n'est événement, ni d'amour ni de guerre,
> Que cet art n'ait enfin appris à tous les yeux.

'You smile,' he continued, 'at my French, or perhaps at my too great ardour of nationality, when speaking of our old masters, and the respect with which I view the efforts of some of my living countrymen; for if you have some good names in England, we too have our Wappers, our Verbeckhoeven, De Keysers, Navez, the Braekeleer, the Paelinck, and the Van Hanselaere, and more, who make worthy essays to maintain the celebrity of our bold and truthful national school. The history of Flemish art is that also of discovery itself. Both Vasari, himself a painter, and the historian Guicciardini, attribute to us that of painting upon glass, and of carrying it to the highest degree of perfection; in which art Von Hort, a citizen of Antwerp, distinguished himself above all others.

'M. de Reiffenberg has proved, against the assertions of Heylen, the justice of the Flemish claims on this point, anterior to the reign of Charles V. Van Eyck was the inventor of a coloured glass of an extraordinary strength and vividness, subsequently introduced into France, and in the sixteenth century into Italy. Who has not admired the sombre beauty, the grand reflected lights of the glass in St. Gudule at Brussels, painted by Jean Ack, of Antwerp, by Jean Floris, and by Diepenbeeck? The beautiful specimens at Tongerloo, and other places, which show the triumph of this art, are scarcely inferior; but so eagerly were they sought by other nations that Belgium was soon deprived of her earliest and finest products. Those of Hoefnagel carried a high price, and were preferred by judges to those of the Dutch Van Donder, or the Volsaks of Germany. Miniature, in fact, was long perfected to admiration in Flanders, while in France and other countries it was a mere cold exhibition of raw colours. It is still more indisputable that Belgium and the world are indebted to Van Eyck for the grand discovery of painting in oil. Certain methods, indeed, of applying oils to paintings were known; but the grand art of mingling and using them so as to produce new results was Van Eyck's; that of carrying it to perfection was due to Jean de Bruges.'

ON A LADY PLAYING
(LADY WALLSCOURT)

By Barry Cornwall

I

Once more amongst those rich and golden strings
Wander with thy white arm, dear lady pale ;
And when at last from thy sweet discourse springs
The aërial music, like the dreams that veil
Earth's shadows with diviner thoughts and things,
Oh, let the passion and the time prevail !
Oh, bid thy spirit thro' the mazes run !
For music is like love—and must be won !

II

Oh, wake the rich chords with thy delicate fingers !
Oh, loose the enchanted Music from mute sleep !
Methinks the fine Phantasma near thee lingers,
Yet will not come, unless tones strong and deep
Compel him—Ah ! methinks (as love-avengers.
Requite upon the heads of those who weep
The sorrows which they gave) the sullen thing
Deserts thee, as thou left'st the vanquish'd string.

III

No—no—it comes, sweeter than death or life,
Sweeter than hope, or joy beneath the moon ;
Sweeter than all is that harmonious strife,
From whose embrace is born a perfect tune,
Where every varying note with thought is rife.
Now—bid thy tender voice enchant us soon,
With whatsoe'er thou wilt—with love—with fears,
The rage of passion, or the strength of tears.

THE LADY WALLSCOURT.

By Sir Thomas Lawrence, P.R.A.

NOTES OF A SPANISH RAMBLE, IN THE SUMMER OF 1839

BY LORD JOHN MANNERS

[*Reprinted by permission of His Grace the Duke of Rutland, K.G.*]

IT was now the end of July, and as our Rambles in Spain were soon to be concluded, we determined to leave our comfortable quarters at Oñate, but were not a little puzzled which way to bend our steps. Zaraetegui and Madrazo had advised us by all means to make an incursion into Navarre, and hinted at the probability of some real fighting taking place in that province in a few days. On the other hand, Don Sebastian and the Duke of Grenada had invited the whole court to a week's festivities at Azpeitia ; and Prince Carini and the young Frenchman pressed us to accompany them thither. After some hesitation, however, we decided in favour of Navarre ; and accordingly, after dinner, on Monday, the 29th of July, mounted our mules and started, under a scorching sun, on our way to Estella, in which town Elio had fixed his quarters. A beautiful ride of two hours brought us to the brow of Sierra de Aralar,[1] whence a magnificent view over a rich plain, glowing with the harvest, and studded with

---

[1] A high chain of mountains, separating Guipuzcoa from the kingdom of Navarre.

villages and hamlets, burst upon us. Two hours more sufficed to bring us down into a noble forest of oaks, Spanish chesnut-trees, and ilexes, in which, just as the evening shades began to prevail, we contrived to lose our way. The muleteer, however, made a fortunate cast, and we reached Alsasua, the first Navarrese village, in due course of time, only, alas! to be disappointed, for we had intended to rest here for the night, and Alsasua possessed no inn. Madrazo, however, who, with Zaraetegui, had preceded us by a day, had left a note for us in charge of the officer in command, advising us to proceed to Iturmendi, a league farther on, where we should find a posada, and to join them the next morning at Aranaz. The officer insisted on our taking two of his lancers to Iturmendi, one by way of escort, to protect us against all Christinos and other ill-disposed persons, and one to go on in front and order supper; so, when we arrived at the posada, very satisfactory preparations were being made in the kitchen, and a blazing wood fire looked very cheery and comfortable after our long ride in the chill night air. The supper was good, the sheets clean, and the beds flealess; and sorry enough was I to be routed up at half-past four the next morning, in order to join our friends at Aranaz in good time.

A fat paymaster, or chief of the commissariat, I am not sure which, in a striped calico jacket, with a huge pair of pistols in his holsters, accompanied us on our road, which lay through the valley of the Borunda, perhaps one of the most fertile valleys in the world. Although war, in its worst shape—civil war—had been raging now for well-nigh six years, and neighbouring Pamplona could send out its bands of harvest-burners, with but small chance of being foiled in their work of destruction, still every inch of ground was cultivated with the greatest care; and the tall Indian corn was waving half-way up the mountains on either side of the valley. At every half-mile, also, a neat village sent out its women and boys to the rich harvest. Nothing, indeed, astonished us more in the whole of our trip than the high state of cultivation of the country. It was only when we got to the frontiers of the Carlist territory that any signs of war presented themselves; and even there the peasants would go about their accustomed labours, while elsewhere peace and plenty seemed to reign securely.

We arrived at Aranaz soon after the appointed hour, but found our friends did not intend to start until after their midday siesta, and that we were all to dine together at their host's, the chief proprietor in the place. In the meantime we witnessed a very curious operation—viz., thrashing out the corn. A large space is cleared and made ready by the roadside; into this the sheaves are brought, and spread out in circles; in the centre of each circle stands a woman, armed with a long goad, or whip, by the constant application of which she keeps in full trot two or three ponies, harnessed to a couple of rough boards, that are studded underneath with pieces of sharp iron. The sheaves are thus in a short time reduced to powder, which is then raked up, and the wheat separated from the chaff by the very simple process of tossing them both in the air by a kind of trident. The chaff is, of course, whisked away to a distance by the wind, and the wheat falls to the ground; this again is passed through a sieve, and the business is completed. The straw, it is true, is pulverised almost into nothing, but it is not altogether lost, for most of it is afterwards collected, and given to the horses and mules, which are said to be very fond of it.

Soon after twelve we sat down to dinner: the party consisted of Zaraetegui and Madrazo, who took the head of the table, our fat friend of the commissariat, the *curá* of the village, a friend of his, our host, and ourselves. As this was the best specimen of a Spanish dinner I had an opportunity of seeing, I will give a short account of it. First of all came a course of lettuces and salads ; then the *sopa*, followed by a great dish of peas (the yellow *gervansos*), and an equally formidable one of beans. Next came the never-failing olio—a capital dish, consisting of pieces of boiled beef, or mutton, with potatoes and a few *gervansos*, and little bits of bacon, with a sprig or so of rich sausage by way of seasoning. Then followed several *entrées* of chicken, &c., all good in their way ; especially an omelet of marrow and other funny materials. To these succeeded the second course—pigeons and fowls ; and then, miserably out of place, a dish of most delicious fresh-caught trout : stewed pears, and other sweets concluded the feast. The wine was of Navarre, considerably stronger, and less pig-skinny than any we had yet met with ; and after our coffee, some most undeniable pale brandy, with an aniseed flavour, was produced.

I sat next to the general, who not only played a remarkably good knife and fork himself, but was bent upon seeing me do the same, and accordingly kept loading my plate with the various good things in a very overpowering manner. Altogether it was a very amusing dinner ; for, though Zaraetegui spoke only Spanish, he could talk about Byron and Washington Irving. Madrazo was talkative and agreeable ; he was with Sir John Moore at Coruña ; and, at the raising of the royal standard in 1833, was in command of the royal guards, which was also the regiment of Zumalacarregui, Goni, Zaraetegui, Sanz, and other distinguished Carlists.

In the cool of the evening we set off in grand style ; seven cavalleros, a dozen troopers, and a score of foot-soldiers. This was the first and last time during our trip that an escort was really necessary. That it was so now the first village we passed through gave witness, for it had been entered during the night by a band of Christinos (said

to be two thousand strong) from Pamplona, who had carried
off the wife of the last year's *alcalde*.

> 'Tis thus they sally out to pillage
> The hen-roost of some peaceful village;
> And while their neighbours were in bed
> A hapless dame away have led.

Our friends surmised that the fat chief of the commissariat was the object of this incursion ; and if so, as he had slept within a few doors of us, what a mercy we were not routed up in the middle of last night, and hurried away to Pamplona ! We left the high road, and, riding through the field on which these nocturnal heroes had halted and formed previously to entering the village, turned aside into a rough horse-track, which, after a long and toilsome ascent, brought us to the top of a very high mountain. Just as we reached the summit, an eagle, scared by our approach, wheeled away majestically into the heavens, while the view over the rich *merindals* of fair Navarre was magnificent. Something very like smoke was descried in the plain beneath, and occasioned a good deal of discussion, some averring it to be the smoke of a hapless village undergoing the tender mercies of the Christinos, others opining it was only fog, to which latter opinion, I must say, I leaned. The descent was pronounced to be so dangerous that we were all made to dismount and entrust our mules to the care of themselves and the soldiers. What a picturesque appearance our party made ! The officers in front with their gold-tasselled *boynas* and shaggy *zumarras* ; the mules with their noses almost touching the ground, carefully picking out their way ; some of the troopers leading and coaxing their startled horses ; others, more bold, remaining in their saddles ; the agile foot-soldiers, in their 'sandal shoon,' with their light muskets swung behind them, now jumping, like mountain goats, from crag to crag, and now belabouring, with many a rattling c——o, a refractory mule ; all winding down, in

E

irregular march, the steep defile, with their arms gleaming and glittering in the blaze of a July sunset. At eight o'clock we entered Ollo, a little village girt round with mountains, in which we meant to pass the night. It was, as may be supposed, no easy matter to find quarters for us all; but, such was the good-will and hospitality shown that, after some consultation between the *curá* and the *alcalde*, they were secured, and at ten o'clock we sat down to a most capital supper, in the house of the latter. A merrier party I never was at, and the *curá* was the life and soul of it—eating for two, drinking for a dozen, girding at the *Ingleses* as *borrachos*, drunkards, which seemed to be the idea generally entertained of us in these parts; anathematising the French, against whom he had borne arms in the war of the constitution, and cutting jokes innumerable, and to me, alas! unintelligible. Opposite him sat a grey-headed patriarch, who inquired eagerly after 'Sir Cotton,' Lord Combermere, who had been quartered for some time in his house, and would seem to have filled the unsophisticated inhabitants of Ollo with wonderment at the magnificence of his dressing-case and plate. After supper the *curá*, the very bodily impersonation of Friar Tuck, insisted on being measured against Granby and myself; but, alas for the pride of Ollo! we both beat him, and while he confessed himself vanquished, the laughing damsels who had waited at table exclaimed it was the first time they had seen taller men than their *curá*, and to think that they should be heretic Englishmen!

While we were waiting for supper accounts were brought to Zaraetegui of the action, such as it was, of the preceding night; by which it appeared that the capture of the ex-*alcalde's* wife did not go altogether unavenged, for, before the marauders had got well out of the fastnesses, the Carlists had collected in considerable numbers, though still inferior to their enemies, and, from the character of the ground, and their intimate knowledge of it, had occasioned them some loss. They killed thirty of the Zaragossa regiment, called *el negro*, the black, which neither gave nor received quarter. As Pamplona was but a few miles distant, we did not retire to rest without some apprehensions of a visit from its 'martial men,' so our mules were kept saddled and bridled, and scouts were placed on the look-out in the dreaded direction. The gentlemen, however, had either been sickened by their reception last night, or wist not that so rich a prize was, as it were, in their clutches. We therefore rose at daybreak, free to continue our march. The sunrise lights on the wooded mountains we had now to ascend were most beautiful : and as the day wore on, and we descended into the hot and scorched plain, I sighed for shade of the stately oaks and beeches we had left behind ; for, however well vines and olives may sound in poetry, they are in sober truth but sorry substitutes for homelier trees, and afford no shade to weary travellers. Estella, which we reached before noon, is built partially on a rock, at the end of a rich valley, through which the Ega, a broad green river, flows, and is the largest and most thriving town I saw during our trip. As the capital of Carlist Navarre, it naturally possessed considerable importance, and its trade seemed very brisk. The country immediately round it is one fertile garden, and the Estella *tomatos* have acquired a Dunstable lark sort of reputation. In the afternoon Granby and I walked by the green river's side for a mile or so, until we discovered a sheltered nook, as we fondly thought, to bathe in ; but, to our great dismay, we had not nearly completed our toilet, when, with slow and measured tread, a whole friary of 'orders brown' marched by. Madrazo, who, with Zaraetegui, had taken up their abode in a friend's house, brought Elio, the Captain-General of Navarre, to call on us in the evening. The latter realised my notion of a *preux-paladin* of chivalry ; strikingly handsome, tall, and well-made, with the best blood of Navarre in his veins, the idol of his soldiers, and the dread of his foes, uniting the most daring personal bravery with great modesty and humanity, this young hero fully justified by his conduct and fidelity the confidence reposed in him by his master. The noble manner in which he rejected all Maroto's offers, and hastened to protect, at the risk of his own life, the person of his king, in the hour of danger, when hearts were failing, and no one knew whom to trust, have rendered his name one which the loyal Navarrese, and all to whom loyalty and valour are still dear, 'will not willingly let die.' Our good *padrona* was lost in wonderment at so great an event as a visit from '*el general*' to any inmates of her house; 'such a thing had never happened to her before,' and she thought it might never happen again, so she bustled backwards and forwards into the room, and out of it, every five minutes. Elio pressed us to stay some days, adding that, as Diego Leon persisted in his cowardly system of burning the harvest, and answered his remonstrances with insolence, he was straining every nerve to come to a decisive action, and expected to succeed in doing so in less than a week. When we had refused his invitation, which we were forced to do from want of time, he insisted on sending an aide-de-camp in the morning to conduct us to the lines at Dicastello, whence we should be able to form a good idea of the theatre of war in Navarre. Accordingly, at five o'clock on the morning of the 1st of August, Eraso, a handsome, noble-looking young man, presented himself at the door, and we set out under his guidance; his father, as is well known, signalised his devotion to the cause by resigning the chief command, to which he was fully entitled, in favour of Zumalacarregui. We passed by the church which had witnessed the execution of the ill-fated generals in February '38; but, as this is not the place for attempting to clear up the mystery which hangs over that transaction, I will only here add that our buxom landlady, who looked the picture of good-humour and kindliness, averred that, with the exception of Carmona, who was much liked, the fate of none of the generals was lamented in Estella. I happened to mention this, some time afterwards, to Madrazo, upon which he shook his head, and said Carmona was the worst because the cleverest of them all.

Our road lay along a line of low hills, forming the bounds of the Carlist territories; the plain country being all more or less in the hands of the Christinos. As far as the eye could reach, nothing in the shape of vegetation, save thirsty-looking olives and dwarf vines, was to be seen,[1] and the sun was most oppressively hot. A ride of two hours brought us to Dicastello, near which I, being the last, was twice asked by women whether Eraso, who was prancing on in front on a high-mettled charger, was not *el general*, in tones indicative of such awe and anxiety that I could not refrain from laughing.

Dicastello is built on the farthest point of the above mentioned range of hills, and from Elio's house we commanded a most extensive view over the plains of Navarre, up to the dimly-seen mountains of Aragon and New Castile in the distance. It was in that part of the plain close to the town that Elio gained his last victory; and an intelligent French officer, who had been fourteen years in the Spanish service, now gave us the details; from which it appeared that, on the night of the 17th of July, a thousand Christino troopers, each carrying a foot-soldier behind him, rode out of Larraga, with the intention of burning the harvest of as many villages as they could. Dicastello was the first place they honoured with their notice, and, on approaching it, the foot-soldiers jumped off, and proceeded to make a feeble attempt against the town, while the troopers set fire to the fields. The Carlists easily beat back

[1] The corn was now all housed; all at least that had escaped the midnight torches of the Christinos.

the assailants, and, in the confusion of the retreat, two companies managed to steal unobserved into a vineyard on the left of the Christino horse, and pour in a volley; this threw them into confusion, and a charge from the Carlist cavalry, four hundred strong, speedily decided the action, such as it was. This, I believe, had been the character of all the actions in Biscay and Navarre for the preceding six months. The energies of both parties were almost exhausted, and, like worn-out gladiators, they painfully stood their ground, gazing on one another, and every now and then aiming a feeble and ineffectual blow at their adversary. Twenty thousand pounds would have given an overwhelming preponderance to either side. The Frenchman was very conversable, and spoke his mind on most subjects so freely that I thought I might venture to ask his opinion of Maroto; but no; at the mention of that dreaded name, he sank his voice into a whisper, and, with a hurried glance at the Spaniards who were conversing in a group hard by, 'begged to be excused, as he made it a rule never to talk on that subject.' Maroto most certainly had acquired a wonderful influence when, at the mention of his name, a talkative Frenchman, attached to another army, and separated from his by mountains and rivers, grew silent and reserved; my wonder is, not that he succeeded in bringing over so many regiments with him, but that he failed in bringing them all. As to Diego Leon, our friend declared he was a perfect brute, with no one redeeming good quality, save that of brute courage; and as, previously to the breaking out of the war, they had been for some years in the same regiment, I suppose he spoke from personal experience. Indeed, nothing could be more contemptuous than the way in which he expressed himself of the Christinos; whose utmost exploit was sallying out on a pillaging expedition from some walled town, and returning thither again. 'But, alas!' said he, 'what can be more miserable than my life here? Only a few of my brother-officers can speak French; nearly all of them are profoundly illiterate; and as for society, there is none! In the winter, to be sure, we get a little snipe-shooting; but otherwise, unless the Christinos take pity on me, and give us something to do, I am without amusement of any kind.'

Of Elio he spoke in high terms, saying he had but one fault—he was too brave, and exposed his person too much. Dicastello had been entered last year by the Christinos, and the general's house, by its still black and naked walls, gave sure tokens of their friendly visit. Having seen what was to be seen, and heard what was to be heard, we returned to Estella; and, after dinner, having bade adieu to our kind friends, Madrazo and Zaraetegui, started, by a different road from that we had come by, for Oñate. Our path lay through a most picturesque valley, by the side of the green Ega; at one time overshadowed by magnificent crags, rising straight over our heads, at another winding through groves of huge old oaks and beeches, and holm oaks. Out of one of these groves we emerged into a most perfect natural amphitheatre, as regular as though it had been formed by art; and on the further side of the hills that encircled it in our front, lay Seudidi, our destined place of rest. The posada, perched on a broad ledge of rock, overhanging the river, presented, as we made our way into it, a most strange appearance. In the low stable on the ground-floor of the inn, which resembled in its arrangements a stable-booth at Ascot races, there must have been from thirty to forty mules and ponies; while men, women, and children—pigs, dogs, cats, and fowls—swearing, laughing, grunting, barking, mewing, and cackling, were huddled together upstairs and downstairs, in most admired confusion. With great difficulty we procured a room, with a sconce stuck into the handle of the door by way of a candle, which had the double merit of giving no light if the door was closed, and flickering in the wind and going out occasionally if it was open. We begged for some supper, which was a weary time ere it appeared. In the next room, a good deal of groaning and tumbling about was going on, and I began to fear that its unfortunate occupant was sick, or dying, when, lo and behold! the door was suddenly thrown open, and a buxom, hearty-looking dame emerged, vociferating, in the loudest tones, that of all the vile holes she ever had been in, this was the vilest; and, in order to prove that she had reason for what she said, she insisted on our inspecting the couch on which she had so restlessly been trying to rest. We did so, and the sight that met our eyes was most unnaturally shocking—a living, moving bed! The lady called for her mule, paid her reckoning, and went on her way, leaving us to a night of misery, such as I never spent before, and hope I shall never spend again.

The supper, consisting of delicious trout, that had jumped out of the river not an hour since, but quite spoiled and made uneatable by the nauseous rancid oil with which they had been drenched, and new-laid eggs, at length appeared. The inn possessed but one glass, as all the others had been carried off by the Christinos during Rodil's incursion—I think our *padrona* said in '34—and she had not thought it worth while to replace them.

Now came the nervous duty of preparing for the night. In an adjoining room were three beds; but after the specimens we had seen of the Seudidi *pulgas* and *chinchas*,[1] none of us were disposed to take them upon trust. Ranelagh declared he would sleep on the heavy oak table, off which we had supped, and with considerable labour we effected its removal; upon this he spread the sheets, and lay down. Granby, after a minute inspection, with the deliberation and courage of a martyr, undressed and turned in; while I, more timid, spread my cloak outside the bed, and rolling

[1] Fleas and their cousins.

myself, clothes and all, up in it, blew out the light. I had
hardly done so when Ranelagh started up, swearing his
couch was so hard and so cold that patience could endure
no longer, and that he should lie on the floor ; so up we
got, and, with a deal of tugging and hauling in the dark,
lugged the disgraced table out of the room, and Ranelagh
deposited his sheets and himself on the floor, pretty nearly
filling up the void between the beds. What possessed us I
don't know, for it was surely no laughing matter ; but laugh
we did, till we could laugh no more ; at length peace was
restored, Ranelagh fell audibly asleep, and I began to enter-
tain some faint hopes, *malgrado* the fleas, who now began
to make themselves felt, of doing the same. But no ! it
was now Granby's turn ; he had been mercilessly punished
for his temerity, and finding, beyond a doubt, that the
place was too hot to hold him, arose, like a troubled spirit,
and proceeded to lay his lacerated body by the side of his
peacefully reposing fellow-traveller. Now, although we
had seen nothing which could excite a suspicion as to the
honest intentions of any of our numerous fellow-lodgers,
still the wild and uncouth aspect of the place, and the
mere fact of there being some thirty or forty people
quartered in and about the house, rendered it prudent for
us to be on our guard, and Ranelagh had laid his pistols by
his side, with a determination to be quick in using them if
required. I foresaw what would happen : after a stumble
or two, stump went Granby on Ranelagh's nose ; a hasty
grunt, in Spanish, was as hastily followed by the click of a
pistol, and Heaven knows what might have followed had
not Granby sung out most lustily in English. Sleep was
now out of the question, and I lay on my 'vermin-couch,'
tumbling and tossing, suffering the pains of purgatory
until the first blush of dawn, when Granby and I hurried
down the rocks, at the risk of our necks, to the brawl-
ing river, and in its icy water forgot the miseries of

the most miserable night it was ever my misfortune to spend.

The fresh morning air, after our bracing bathe, was delicious, as we worked our way up to the Amescoas through picturesque beech-woods, overhanging the valley. The Amescoas are great uneven plains, at the summit of an extensive chain of hills, partly covered with forests, with large clear portions of grass, and rocks here and there. Our road lay through that part of them in which Zumalacarregui so completely defeated Valdez's large and well-appointed army; and it was from the top of the pass which took us down into the Borunda that, on the afternoon of the 22nd of April, 1835, his two sentinels descried the Christino masses, twenty thousand strong, slowly and carelessly winding up the gorge of the valley, and commencing the toilsome ascent. Most commanders would, I think, have been tempted, from the great facilities it affords of destroying an ascending army, to dispute the pass; but the wary hero had laid a deeper and a safer plan. Immediately and silently, and without being observed, he withdrew his men to the furthest thickets of the Amescoas, and there lay concealed, while his unsuspecting victims were carousing in their mountain bivouac after their painful march, until, at the dead of night, when all were buried in security and slumber, he precipitated himself on them. An utter dispersion followed, and in an hour's time the army of the boastful Valdez had ceased to exist.

We dismounted, and descended into the Borunda on foot, but the sun was too powerful to allow much walking, and very thankful was I when, at half-past ten, we entered the wood on the other side of the Alsagua, in which we had lost our way in the beginning of the week. Here we met a regiment marching to Elio's quarters; the men were looking hot and distressed and foot-sore, but many were singing, and all seemed tolerably well clothed and well fed, though, to be sure, some of the officers would not have been the worse for new uniforms. We were told they were a Cantabrian regiment, which Maroto had exchanged for the Navarrese Guides, with Elio, as Espartero had been offering very seductive reasons to induce them to return to their homes at Santander, &c.; subsequent events, however, make me, I confess, very sceptical as to Maroto's motives. An hour's ride through the wood brought us to a river, by the bank of which we unburthened our mules, and made preparations for a comfortable dinner and siesta. The indiarubber wine-flask was popped under a large stone in the river, and while we bathed the muleteer tried, but in vain, to tickle some trout. At midday we sat down to our simple dinner, *patulæ sub tegmine fagi*, with prodigious appetites, and found, to our great delight, that the cold running stream had most effectually iced the wine, so that our only sorrow was that the flask held no more than it did. Then came an hour's grateful and flealess slumber, under the beechen shade, and we resumed our march to Oñate; but, instead of re-crossing the mountains we had travelled before, we kept the plain until we had nearly reached Segura, and then turned up to the left, by some iron mines, which extend along nearly the whole side of the Sierra de Mutiloa, and are very productive. Their wild unearthly-looking inhabitants came out of their dens and caverns to gaze in surprise at us as we wound up the mountain; in truth, the path we had taken was very little frequented, and these Titans were all unaccustomed to strangers; more perfect 'salvages' I never beheld, and yet they, too, had a kind word and greeting for the travellers. It was after ten o'clock ere we found ourselves established once more, and for the last time, in our snug lodgings at Oñate, having been journeying for seventeen hours. Our fair hostess astonished us with the news that the King, having returned from the festivities of Azpeitia, started almost immediately, with his whole court, for Tolosa, whither we must follow him if we wished to pay our respects to him before leaving his kingdom. Whether this sudden step was taken from an inkling of the treason that was working around him, and a consequent anxiety to be nearer that friendly prison-house, France, I know not; but we were told that, ever since Rodil's memorable pursuit of him, in 1834, the King had been in the habit of moving from place to place at an hour's notice, and the Queen and her ladies were frequently put to no small inconvenience from the brief time allowed them to prepare for their departure. Be this as it may, the royal bird had flown, and Oñate, in consequence, resembled a city of the dead. Not being able to find four mules in time, we remained the next day in this 'deserted village'; and, truth to say, I was not sorry to get one day's rest after our racketing excursion into Navarre. In the evening, the two good priests, having heard of our return, came to pay us a farewell visit, and the communicative one told a curious anecdote of his fellow-townsman, Raymon Cabrera, whom he worshipped with an intensity of adoration that would have, in these dull, unheroic days, delighted even the hero-worshipping Thomas Carlyle. 'Once, not long after the commencement of hostilities, the chieftain's band, in those days mustering barely one hundred men, was entirely dispersed, and he found himself, with two companions, wandering wearily and hungrily among his native mountains. He soon got tired of this vagrancy, and hit on the following bold expedient for revictualling himself and reassembling his band. It was midday, and he turned to his companions, ordering one to approach in one direction, and the other in another, a little village called Lledo, in the plain below them, and to keep firing off their guns at intervals, while he himself would march straight up to the *alcalde's* house. So it turned out: he rapped fiercely at the *alcalde's* door; *bang* on the right! another thundering rap at the door; *bang* on the left! "*Valgame Dios!*" cries the frightened mayor, starting up from his troubled siesta;

"who's there? What do you want?" More shots, and Cabrera answers—"'Tis the advanced guard; Cabrera (even then a dreaded name) must have rations for two hundred men left, by such an hour in the evening, in the forest hard by, or—you know the alternative!" No more is said, and the rations are provided. Cabrera soon found himself at the head of his former followers, and his band,

> One by one, and two by two,
> Into a mighty squadron grew,

until now, on him and his movements, are bent the eyes of thousands, and the fisherman's son, the sacristan of Tortosa, the Count of Morella, upholds, almost singly, the high and holy cause of loyalty and religion in Spain.'[1]

When I told the priest that we were about to go into Switzerland, he seemed for some time incredulous, and, opening his eyes very wide, exclaimed '*hombre!*' several times. At last he asked, 'Why Switzerland? what good can you do the cause there?' so fully persuaded was he, as well as others, that our visit was not one of pure curiosity. As we intended to start very early the next morning, in order to reach Tolosa ere midday, we bade adieu to our kind *padrona* over-night; and there was something very mournful and prophetic in the tone of her voice, as she hoped that, if the Christinos succeeded, and she was forced to leave her home and fly to England, we would not forget our *séjour* at Oñate. Heaven knows what was her fate, when, in less than a month from the time, Oñate was delivered into the hands of the Christinos.

It was pitch dark when, at three o'clock in the morning of the 4th of August, we left Oñate, and a pretty constant drizzle for the first three hours gave promise of a rainy day; but no; it cleared up, and we had neither sun, nor rain, nor dust, to molest us during the remainder of our

---

[1] This was written just before the conclusion of the war.

march. In a little village, not far from Villafranca, in the middle of a moderately-sized garden, stands the modest white-washed cottage in which Zumalacarregui was born; his widow was living there. Villafranca, a curious old walled town, still bore marks of the vigorous manner in which the hero besieged it, many of the houses being quite riddled with shots, and part of the wall in a most dilapidated state. This was, I believe, the first fortified town taken by Zumalacarregui, and the famous 'Grandfather' constituted his park of artillery. We arrived at Tolosa before midday, and in the evening sauntered about the town, which presented a much gayer appearance than it did the first time we entered it. Its *paseos* (for Tolosa boasts two) were crowded, and under the trees, to the pipe and tabor, lads and lasses were tripping lightsomely along, to the same measure as we had seen danced at Oñate, but with more spirit, while the *señoras* and *caballeros* walked gravely up and down the shady avenues, ever and anon pausing in front of some merry group, and applauding their joyous movements. Here we fell in with Señor Ramirez de la Pescina,[1] and several other friends, and, adjourning with them to the Tolosa Gunter's, discussed, over some capital ices, the merits of the duke's and Lord Clarendon's speeches, which the last post had brought.

Monday, 5th.—I managed to-day to talk a little Spanish to Starico, Count Casa d'Eguia's nephew, who assured me that the troops had not received any pay for the last eight months, and seemed, very naturally, to anticipate the worst consequences therefrom. Maroto's designs were now drawing near their fulfilment. In the course of the day I bought some boynas and Carlist buttons, as souvenirs of the provinces at the shop of a good lady who was in St. Sebastian when the legionities entered, but escaped out of it subsequently. She affirmed—with perfect truth, I dare say—

[1] At that time Secretary of State and Despatch.

that the men were *muy ordinarios*, but allowed some of the officers to be *finos*, and of *grandes casas*.

After the evening ices we proceeded to the palace—much the same kind of house as that at Oñate, but a little larger—to pay our farewell respects to their majesties. While we were waiting to be introduced to their presence, Señers Erro and Villareal came, and talked to us. From the former we learned that the harvest, which had just been got in, was unusually plenteous, and that they had still in the provinces cattle and sheep sufficient for carrying on the war four or five more years. Their majesties received us as affably as they had done on the former occasion, but the young prince was not present. The King's laugh is a peculiar one, and not easy to be described. Having thanked him most sincerely for the great kindness and hospitality we had encountered in every part of his mountain kingdom, from high and low, and taken leave of Señor Ramirez and other friends, we retired to our flea-inhabited couches.

Tuesday, 6th.—Up at daybreak: obliged, for the first time since crossing the Pyrenees, to object to the bill: for seventeen douros was too exorbitant a demand; and our landlady, after some opposition and much grumbling, consented to take thirteen. This important point settled, we started with Prince Carini and Count de Blacas for the lines—the famous lines of Andoain. At Villabona, General ———'s head-quarters, we stopped, and procured a capital cicerone in the person of his aide-de-camp, Captain Vial, under whose guidance we made a complete tour of the lines, which are triple, and entirely command the Hernani road. They were finished two years ago, by the Carlists, under the superintendence of German artillery officers, and appeared to my unpractised, unmilitary eye, to be very perfect. Vial, from one of the highest positions, gave an animated account of the action which dispossessed the Christinos of them, and inveighed with much warmth on the spirit of wanton cruelty which actuated them in their retreat to set fire to the cottages of the helpless peasantry, in which they had been living. But more eloquent than his words were the still black and roofless hamlets themselves.

The Christino fort of Santa Barbara, crowning a hill a few miles off, was glittering in the sun, and with the aid of a telescope I was able to discover St. Sebastian in the distance to the right. Having seen what was to be seen, and taken leave of our companions, we turned our mules towards France, and speedily struck into the same mountain track we had travelled a month ago, on our entrance into Spain. About noon we reached the same pleasant chestnut-grove, on the brow of the hills, under which we had then dined; nor did we this time lose so favourable an opportunity of discussing the chickens and hard-boiled eggs we had brought from Tolosa. I thought the scenery, as we rode along the mountain-tops, still more magnificent than when, for the first time, I gazed down upon St. Sebastian; and, ere we commenced descending into the dell in which Goyzueta is situated, we turned to take 'one last fond look' at as glorious a picture of mountain and wood and valley, with the blue white-crisped sea beyond, and the still bluer sky above, as eye ever lighted on. Presently we fell in with a roving party of *voluntarios*; and now, for the first time, we might have perceived signs of lawlessness and insubordination—harbingers of the storm which was soon to burst—in the promising offer one of them made to the sturdy muleteer, of a pesetto for Ranelagh's sword, which he was carrying. Nothing unpleasant, however, ensued; and they proceeded on their way into the interior, and we, on our part, reached Goyzueta at five o'clock without let or hindrance. I bathed, for the last time, in Spanish waters, in the Urumea, which rises in the mountains which surround the village, and produced some most delicious trout for our early supper, after which we speedily turned into the coarse but clean beds, as we had strictly charged the muleteers to call us at half-past two next morning. This, however, they did not do, alleging—perhaps with reason—that the frontiers were in so disturbed a state, that it would not have been safe to travel before daybreak; and so it was four ere we sallied forth from Goyzueta. The morning breeze, wafted from the sea, was exquisitely fresh, and the sun was rising magnificently among the mountains, while the hundred different sorts of fern and heath, and brightly-coloured wild flowers, and long dank grasses were gleaming and glistening and sending out their sweetest odours under the heavy dew—heavy enough, to my certain knowledge, for at one time sleep so completely overpowered me that I was forced, in order to escape falling off, to quit my mule and walk for a mile or so. The maize—which is not cut till October—was growing luxuriantly in the valley, or rather dell, in which stands Vera; and I observed a good deal of balm-mint between its long stalks. We rode into Vera between eleven and twelve o'clock, and found our buxom *padrona* delighted to see us again; and, although some *peseteros* had menaced the village only the day before, and so alarmed the inhabitants that they had removed most of their chattels to a place of safety, she instantly brought out the hats which we had entrusted to her, and busied herself in preparing as good a dinner for the *tres Ingleses* as her *cuisine* could produce. As it was a fast-day she had no meat to offer us, but the most voracious Protestant that ever breathed need not have grumbled at the fish-dinner we sat down to. There were lettuces, and salad, and the good bread *sopa* and stewed eels, and dressed craw-fish, and trout most fresh and delicate, and new-laid eggs, with very good wine and bread; and then, after dinner, a cup of coffee and glass of right good *aguardiente*—and all for the moderate charge of four shillings and twopence, English money. The commandant of Vera, a funny little man in a round jacket, with sandals

F

on his feet, came after dinner to offer us a couple of his *voluntarios* as an escort, 'for the frontiers,' he said, 'are not just at present very quiet.' They accompanied us, accordingly, to the boundary line; but our only stoppage was by the Carlist custom-house officers, just outside Vera— and a pretty absurd farce this same stoppage was: all the trunks and boxes were taken off, and placed on the grass under the trees, and then, with great gravity and gentleness, did two or three huge wild-looking Carlist soldiers proceed to search for 'papers against the King, and Spanish money.' From the wretched turn affairs were so soon to take, the hunt after the first-mentioned article was, I doubt not, very right and necessary; but, as to Spanish or other money, few people, I imagine, leaving the provinces, were over-burdened in that way, and we certainly were not, for it was with great difficulty that we could scrape together pesetos sufficient to reward our trusty conductors. In spite, however, of all our protestations of loyalty and poverty (too often, alas! convertible terms), search they would, and search they did, and so half an hour was lost in this silly manner. When it was over we proceeded smoothly enough along a beautiful path winding through the bosom of the mountains, until we arrived at the French boundary custom-house. Here our guards left us, and returned to Vera; while we endeavoured, for a minute or two, to brazen the affair out as we best could; but the commissary soon convinced us of the inutility of all such attempts by saying, with a significant smile: 'Oh, gentlemen! don't trouble yourselves; I know you very well: you crossed the frontiers on the night of the 8th of last month, and I have received strict orders to examine all your papers and letters, as you are greatly suspected.'

This was pleasant! but there was no help for it; and Ranelagh remonstrated in vain. We were deprived of our arms, and papers, and passports, and I had the mortification of seeing a letter which a grateful Carlist officer had entrusted me with to deliver to somebody who had been kind to him while an exile in England seized among others I assured the commissary that it was but a letter I was going to put into the post at Bayonne. 'Doubtless,' said he ; 'but the writing is Spanish.' When they had brought their ransacking to a close we were marched off into Urruna, guarded by two *gendarmes*, who informed us we had a narrow escape the night we crossed the Pyrenees, for they had received intelligence as to our movements, and were only twenty minutes behind us. Our faithful muleteers did not at all relish the idea of being marched into a French town like criminals ; and one of them, a perfect giant, and a great wag, made me laugh heartily, in spite of our disconsolate position, by the semi-lugubrious, semi-comical manner in which he pinched my arm, and whispered *prigionero* as we entered the village. It was market-day : and while our carriage was being ferreted out of its hiding-place and made ready for a start, I amused myself by remarking the peculiar costume and burly forms of the French Basque farmers. After a while, the *gendarmes*—who now managed everything—announced that the horses were put to, and, getting up into the dicky behind, we entered the britchska, and off we went. On arriving, at half-past nine, at Bayonne, we were taken before the prefect's secretary, who, in a few minutes, civilly enough dismissed us to tea and to bed. The next day the various things which had been seized were restored to us, and so ended our 'Trip across the Spanish Frontier.'

*THE PLAZA REAL AND THE CATHE-
DRAL, SEVILLE, WITH THE PROCES-
SION OF THE CORPUS CHRISTI
CEREMONY*

By Thomas Roscoe

The Plaza Real, one of the most spacious squares in Seville, contains, among other edifices, the town hall and courts of justice. The corner of the latter is seen to the right, from the point of view chosen by the artist, as represented in the annexed view. The architectural decorations are of the most elaborate description, the work of a celebrated sculptor in the time of the Emperor Charles V. Considered in detail, they are of the most exquisite workmanship; but as a whole the effect is not good, being at variance with all our ideas of simplicity and true taste. In a national view, however, it may be questioned how far our own notions in this respect approach nearer than those of the Moors—assuredly more wild and fanciful—to the ideal of decorative beauty and taste. With all the extravagances and complicated variety of their system, and to whatever singular results it may sometimes lead, the artist, if I may judge from his written opinions, is inclined to give the preference to their principles, which he thinks superior to tameness and uniformity. The houses which surround the Plaza Real are of great antiquity, and assort well with the general aspect of the place, and with the magnificent cathedral by which the view is bounded.

PLAZA REALE, SEVILLE.

By David Roberts, R.A.

Woodbury-Gravure.

The grand ceremony of the Corpus Christi, as it here appears in its most gorgeous array, is known to be one of the most solemn and important of religious festivals. In Seville especially, it is one to which strangers from all parts of Spain eagerly resort, at whatever expense or inconvenience. Over the entire line of streets through which the procession moves awnings are suspended; but these, in the plate before us, the artist, for the sake of showing the noble back-ground, has not introduced. In front of the procession is borne the banner of the cathedral, the staff and decorations of which are of silver and gold. On the flag itself is introduced a representation of the Last Supper. Immediately behind is carried the Mystery of the Potter's Daughters, whose effigies are seen supporting the Giralda. Lest the reader should not be so fortunate as to have met with the history of these two ladies, be it known that they were two of the first, if not the very first, who suffered martyrdom on the introduction of Christianity into this part of Spain. On this account, it is difficult to express the degree of veneration in which they are held throughout their native suburb of the Triana, where the potter himself is esteemed little lower than a saint. During a violent earthquake, that visited Seville and shook the city to its centre, the great tower of the Giralda alone stood firm as a rock. While the consternation of the devoted city was at its height, the two sisters were seen with the utmost coolness and intrepidity shouldering up and steadying the immense pile. In how short a time they had expanded in size proportionable to the tower we are unable to state. The tower itself is three hundred and sixty feet in height, but to attempt to doubt the miracle in Seville might not be wholly prudent even now. It were, perhaps, safer to question the superior science of the Moorish architect, whose miracle of skill still exhibits its proofs to view. Yet these truly conservative ladies obtain all the credit of the work; and, what is more, have a magnificent chapel in the cathedral, which is appropriated to their sole use. On occasion of the ceremony of the Corpus Christi, they are removed with great pomp, together with the representation of the Giralda,[1] and paraded through the city. It is observed by the artist, with a proper respect for the antique, that the effect of their appearing arrayed in the costume of the present day is truly absurd. The mantilla, and head-dress with comb, do not at all agree with our notions of what the potter's daughters must have been. There is another absurdity, scarcely less glaring to those who are not accustomed to Spanish tastes and superstitions. The eyes of the figures are made to roll about by a person concealed underneath pulling a string, so as to make the populace imagine they are in the act of prayer.

Next to these follows the silver *custodia*, containing the sacred host. This is of solid silver, of the most exquisite workmanship; its weight is enormous; and it is moved by sixteen men, who, to give it the appearance of self-motion, are also concealed.

The boys in antique Spanish dresses, in front of the Mystery of the Potter's Daughters, dance before the high altar during mass, both morning and evening, while the festival lasts. This is a privilege granted exclusively to this cathedral by his holiness the Pope, and of which the Sevillians are not a little proud. It is said to be in imitation of David dancing before the ark, only with this difference—the latter played the harp, whereas the former rattle the castanets; how far becoming in a solemn religious ceremony we pretend not to judge.

---

[1] The tower of the cathedral called La Giralda was built by the Moors in 1196. From its summit the muezzin was wont to summon faithful Mahomedans to their prayers. The pinnacle is crowned with a bronze figure of Faith called El Giranditto, which veers in the slightest breeze.

ARAB THIEVES

The following extracts are from the 'Adventures of Giovanni, Finati,' an Italian and a soldier of fortune, who, after having served in the army of Mahomet Ali, acted in the capacity of guide to European travellers in Egypt and Arabia. The great advantages which both these situations afforded him are apparent in his work, which, both for the variety of the incidents it details, and the traits of Eastern manners it contains, is one of the most entertaining and useful of the kind that has been recently published. The work has been translated from the original Italian, by William John Bankes, Esq., formerly M.P., whom he was engaged to attend during his tour in the East, and whose name is a guarantee for the authenticity of the stories, many of which relate to incidents that fell under that gentleman's notice. (*Written in* 1838.)

WE were embarked upon the Nile in barges, which were suffered to drop down the stream, but we occasionally put to shore, either to shelter ourselves from the violent heat of the sun, or to pass the night; and two incidents which happened during those pauses, in the short passage from Manfalloot, may be worth mentioning. Whilst moored at Minieh, one night, preparatory to my going to rest, I had retired to some distance from my companions, on the shore, and was there in no favourable posture for defence: it was dark, but I thought that I could distinguish something moving on the ground near me, which I supposed to be a dog; but a stone which I threw soon discovered my error, for a man started up, and seemed to slink away to a distance, so that I looked no more after him; but, within a very few seconds, I felt him leap suddenly on me from behind, and lay violent hold both of my wrists and of my throat, and so drag me along backwards with him into a pit close at hand, which is filled by the Nile at some seasons, but was then dry. He was a powerful man: and I had no arms whatever upon me for defending myself, so that, keeping me still throttled with one hand, and kneeling on me, he proceeded to rifle me with the other, in search of money, or whatever might be worth his taking; but, finding nothing, he gave me at last a stab in the right shoulder with a little crooked knife which he wore, and, as he loosed me, struck several blows with a stick to prevent my following. I hastened back to the boat, and there, showing my wound, told my comrades what had just happened, upon which all immediately armed themselves and hastened to the spot; but, though so little time had been lost, and they searched for hours together in all directions, no signs of the culprit were discoverable. I had, however, the consolation of knowing that he was without booty, and that the cut which he had given me, though it bled much in the first moments, was of little consequence.

An adventure of this nature had nothing in it that was uncommon at that time—the Egyptian peasantry were become quite a nation of thieves, and had carried their art to a high degree of skill and perfection; in fact, the confusion of the times, and the constant struggles between the Pasha's army and the Mamelukes, had so taken away from them all opportunity for industry or honest gains, as well as all security for property, and had so laid waste the villages and the whole territory, that a better course of life could hardly be expected from them; robberies, therefore, and violences, and even murders, became matters of daily occurrence. We were destined, a little lower down, to witness an act of still greater audacity, and which brought with it far more fatal effects.

We had put to shore near Benysouef, and, after having

dined together at noon in one of the great groves of palm-trees, continued sitting there all the afternoon ; and, to pass the time, were amusing ourselves with games of cards and dice. The stakes were trifling at first, but rose as we proceeded ; and, from playing, at the outset, for paras, we advanced at last to gold. The interest, of course, grew deeper in proportion, and before nightfall some had been winners of considerable sums. The losers were now in no temper to leave off, and so, when it grew dark, lanterns were lighted and hung from the trees, that the game might be continued. This drew several Arab thieves about us, who crept on, little by little, close to our circle, unperceived, for we of ourselves constituted a little crowd, being from thirty to forty soldiers, and were all so engrossed by our play that we never noticed the strangers, but took for granted that all who were standing or sitting round were our own attendants or the boat's crew ; and the light, indeed, which our lanterns gave was hardly sufficient to have undeceived us. Whilst each was sitting with his little heap of money before him, intent upon the cards, which were dealing round at the moment, some of these roguish interlopers suddenly knocked the lights out, and others, at the same instant discharging handfuls of dust into our eyes, snatched up as much of the money as they could lay hold of and made off with it. In the first moment of surprise none of us knew what had happened, and nothing remained to be seen but our own party. Without entering upon any explanation, or giving time for any, there began a general scuffle, everyone in the number supposing himself robbed and insulted by his comrades. All had instant recourse to their arms, which were unfortunately at hand, some stabbing with their dirks, and some cutting with their sabres ; and the confusion and bloodshed proceeded so far that they did not cease till nine of our party lay dead or dying on the ground, and several of the remainder grievously wounded, so that I considered myself fortunate in escaping with only a slight sabre-cut upon the arm. We learned afterwards, from some of the bystanders, when our spirits were calmed and more brought to reason, what it was that had really taken place, and that they had in vain tried to stop our hands in time, and to pacify our misdirected fury at the beginning of the fray. We were filled with shame and remorse; but there was no help for what had happened, so we mourned over our companions and got them buried.

While some of the Mamelukes were encamped about Minieh, a thief set his mind upon carrying off the horse and wearing-apparel of one of their Beys, and with this intention contrived, in the dead of the night, to creep, unperceived, within the tent, where, as it was winter-time, embers were burning and showed the rich clothes of the Bey lying close at hand. The thief, as he squatted down by the fire, drew them softly to him and put them all on; and then, after filling a pipe and lighting it, went deliberately to the tent-door, and, tapping a groom, who was sleeping near, with the pipe-end, made a sign to him for the horse, which stood piquetted in front. It was brought; he mounted and rode off. On the morrow, when the clothes of the Bey could nowhere be found, none could form a conjecture as to what had become of them, until the groom, on being questioned, mentioned to his fellow-servants that their master was not yet returned from his ride, and told them how he had suddenly called for his horse in the night, which at last seemed to give some clue to what had really happened. Upon this the Bey, anxious to recover his horse, as well as curious to ascertain the particulars, ordered it to be published abroad that, if the person who had robbed him would, within two days, bring back what he had taken, he should not only be freely pardoned, but should receive also the full value of the animal and of the suit of clothes.

Relying on the good faith of this promise, and possibly,

too, not a little vain of his exploit, the Arab presented himself, and brought his booty; and the Bey also, on his part, punctually kept his word; but since, besides the loss, there was something in the transaction that placed the Bey in rather a ludicrous light, it went hard with him to let the rogue depart so freely, and he seemed to be considering what he should do; so that, to gain time, he was continually asking over and over again fresh and more circumstantial accounts of the manner in which the stratagem had been conducted. The other was too crafty not to perceive that no good might be preparing for him, and began to feel anxious to get safe out of the scrape. He showed no impatience, however, but entered minutely into every detail, accompanying the whole with a great deal of corresponding action, at one time sitting down by the fire, and making believe as though he were slily drawing on the different articles of dress, so as to throw the Bey himself and all who saw and heard him into fits of laughter. When he came at last to what concerned the horse, 'It was,' he said, 'brought to me, and I leaped upon his back;' and so, in effect, flinging himself again into the saddle, and spurring the flanks sharply with the stirrup-irons, he rode off with all the money that he had received for the animal in his pocket, and had got much too far during the first moments of surprise for any of the bullets to take effect that were fired at him in his flight, and nothing further was ever heard of him or the horse.

THE FAMILY OF SIR WALTER SCOTT

LETTER FROM SIR WALTER SCOTT TO SIR ADAM FERGUSON, DESCRIPTIVE OF A PICTURE PAINTED AT ABBOTSFORD BY DAVID WILKIE, ESQ., R.A.

MY DEAR ADAM,—The picture you mention has something in it of rather a domestic character, as the personages are represented in a sort of masquerade, such being the pleasure of the accomplished painter. Nevertheless, if you, the proprietor, incline to have it engraved, I do not see that I am entitled to make any objection.

But Mr. —— mentions, besides, a desire to have anecdotes of my private and domestic life, or, as he expresses himself, a portrait of the author in his night-gown and slippers ; and this from you, who, I dare say, could furnish some anecdotes of our younger days which might now seem ludicrous enough. Even as to my night-gown and slippers, I believe the time has been when the articles of my wardrobe were as familiar to your memory as Poins's to Prince Henry : but that period has been for some years past, and I cannot think it would be interesting to the public to learn that I had changed my old robe-de-chambre for a handsome douillette when I was last at Paris.

The truth is, that a man of ordinary sense cannot be supposed delighted with the species of gossip which, in the dearth of other news, recurs to such a quiet individual as myself ; and though, like a well-behaved lion of twenty years' standing, I am not inclined to vex myself about what I cannot help, I will not, in any case in which I can prevent it, be accessory to these follies. There is no man known at

Woodbury-Gravure.

SIR WALTER SCOTT AND HIS FAMILY.

By Sir David Wilkie, R.A.

all in literature who may not have more to tell of his private life than I have : I have surmounted no difficulties either of birth or education, nor have I been favoured by any particular advantages, and my life has been as void of incidents of importance as that of the 'weary knife-grinder'—

'Story! God bless you! I have none to tell, Sir.'

The follies of youth ought long since to have passed away ; and if the prejudices and absurdities of age have come in their place, I will keep them, as Beau Tibbs did his prospect, for the amusement of my domestic friends. A mere enumeration of the persons in the sketch is all which I can possibly permit to be published respecting myself and my family ; and, as must be the lot of humanity when we look back seven or eight years, even what follows cannot be drawn up without some very painful recollections.

The idea which our inimitable Wilkie adopted was to represent our family group in the garb of south-country peasants, supposed to be concerting a merry-making, for which some of the preparations are seen. The place is the terrace near Kayside, commanding an extensive view towards the Eildon Hills. 1. The sitting figure, in the dress of a miller, I believe, represents Sir Walter Scott, author of a few scores of volumes, and proprietor of Abbotsford, in the County of Roxburgh. 2. In front, and presenting, we may suppose, a country wag somewhat addicted to poaching, stands Sir Adam Ferguson, Knight, Keeper of the Regalia of Scotland. 3. In the background is a very handsome old man, upwards of eighty-four years old at the time, painted in his own character of a shepherd. He also belonged to the numerous clan of Scott. He used to claim credit for three things unusual among the southland shepherds : first that he had never been *fou* in the course of his life ; secondly, that he never had struck a man in anger ; thirdly, that, though entrusted with the management of large sales of stock, he had never lost a penny for his master by a bad debt. He died soon afterwards at Abbotsford. 4, 5, 6. Of the three female figures the elder is the late regretted mother of the family represented. 5. The young person most forward in the group is Miss Sophia Charlotte Scott, now Mrs. John Gibson Lockhart; and 6, her younger sister, Miss Ann Scott. Both are represented as ewe-milkers, with their *leglins*, or milk-pails. 7. On the left hand of the shepherd, the young man holding a fowling-piece is the eldest son of Sir Walter, now Captain in the King's Hussars. 8. The boy is the youngest of the family, Charles Scott, now of Brazenose College, Oxford. The two dogs were distinguished favourites of the family: the large one was a stag-hound of the old Highland breed, called 'Maida,' and one of the handsomest dogs that could be found; he was a present to me from the chief of Glengary, and was highly valued, both on account of his beauty, his fidelity, and the great rarity of the breed. The other is a little Highland terrier, called *Ourisk* (goblin), of a particular kind, bred in Kintail. It was a present from the Honourable Mrs. Stuart Mackenzie, and is a valuable specimen of a race which is now also scarce. Maida, like Bran, Lerath, and other dogs of distinction, slumbers 'beneath his stone,' distinguished by an epitaph, which, to the honour of Scottish scholarship be it spoken, has only *one* false quantity in *two* lines.

> Maidæ marmorea dormis sub imagine Maida
> Ad januam domini sit tibi terra levis.

If it should suit Mr.—— 's purpose to adopt the above illustrations, he is heartily welcome to them, but I make it my especial bargain that nothing more is said upon them.

It strikes me, however, that there is a story about old Thomas Scott, the shepherd, which is characteristic, and which I will make your friend welcome to. Tom was, both as a trusted servant and as a rich fellow in his line, a person of considerable importance among his class in the neighbourhood, and used to stickle a good deal to keep his place in public opinion. Now, he suffered, in his own idea at least, from the consequence assumed by a country neighbour who, though neither so well reputed for wealth or sagacity as Thomas Scott, had yet an advantage over him, from having seen the late king, and used to take precedence upon all occasions when they chanced to meet. Thomas suffered under this superiority. But after this sketch was finished, and exhibited in London, the newspapers made it known that his present Majesty had condescended to take some notice of it. Delighted with the circumstance, Thomas Scott set out on a most oppressively hot day, to walk five miles to Bowden, where his rival resided. He had no sooner entered the cottage than he called out in his broad forest dialect—'Andro', man, did ye anes *sey* (see) the king?' 'In troth did I, Tam,' answered Andro'; 'sit down, and I'll tell ye a' about it. Ye *sey*, I was at Lonon, in a place they ca' the park, that is no like a hained hog-fence, or like the four-nooked parks in this country——' 'Hout awa,' said Thomas ; 'I have heard a' that before : I only came ower the knowe now to tell you, that, if you have seen the king, the king has seen *mey*' (me). And so he returned with a jocund heart, assuring his friends 'it had done him muckle gude to settle accounts with Andro'.'

Jocere hæc—as the old Laird of Restalrig writes to the Earl of Gowrie ; farewell, my old, tried, and dear friend, of forty long years. Our enjoyments must now be of a character less vivid than those we have shared together,

> But still at our lot it were vain to repine,
> Youth cannot return, or the days of Lang Syne.

Yours affectionately,—WALTER SCOTT.

Abbotsford : August 2, 1827.

THE LADY'S DREAM

WHILE my lady sleepeth,
   The dark-blue heaven is bright ;
Soft the moonbeam creepeth
   Round her bower all night.
Thou gentle, gentle breeze,
   While my lady slumbers,
Waft lightly through the trees,
   Echoes of my numbers,
The dreaming ear to please.

Spanish Serenade.

THE LADY'S DREAM.

By Thomas Stothard, R.A.

TO BE READ AT DUSK

By Charles Dickens

One, two, three, four, five. There were five of them.

Five couriers, sitting on a bench outside the convent on the summit of the Great St. Bernard in Switzerland, looking at the remote heights stained by the setting sun as if a mighty quantity of red wine had been broached upon the mountain-top, and had not yet had time to sink into the snow.

This is not my simile. It was made for the occasion by the stoutest courier, who was a German. None of the others took any more notice of it than they took of me, sitting on another bench on the other side of the convent door, smoking my cigar, like them, and—also like them—looking at the reddened snow, and at the lonely shed hard by, where the bodies of belated travellers, dug out of it, slowly wither away, knowing no corruption in that cold region.

The wine upon the mountain-top soaked in as we looked; the mountain became white; the sky, a very dark blue; the wind rose; and the air turned piercing cold. The five couriers buttoned their rough coats. There being no safer man to imitate in all such proceedings than a courier, I buttoned mine.

The mountain in the sunset had stopped the five couriers in a conversation. It is a sublime sight, likely to stop conversation. The mountain being now out of the sunset they resumed. Not that I had heard any part of their previous discourse; for, indeed, I had not then broken away from the American gentleman, in the travellers' parlour of the convent, who, sitting with his face to the fire, had undertaken to realise to me the whole progress of events which had led to the accumulation by the Honourable Ananias Dodger of one of the largest acquisitions of dollars ever made in our country.

'My God!' said the Swiss courier, speaking in French— which I do not hold (as some authors appear to do) to be such an all-sufficient excuse for a naughty word, that I have only to write it in that language to make it innocent—'if you talk of ghosts——'

'But I *don't* talk of ghosts,' said the German.

'Of what then?' asked the Swiss.

'If I knew of what then,' said the German, 'I should probably know a great deal more.'

It was a good answer, I thought, and it made me curious. So I moved my position to that corner of my bench which was nearest to them, and, leaning my back against the convent-wall, heard perfectly, without appearing to attend.

'Thunder and lightning!' said the German, warming, 'when a certain man is coming to see you, unexpectedly, and, without his own knowledge, sends some invisible messenger, to put the idea of him in your head all day, what do you call that? When you walk along a crowded street— at Frankfort, Milan, London, Paris—and think that a passing stranger is like your friend Heinrich, and then that another passing stranger is like your friend Heinrich, and so begin to have a strange foreknowledge that presently you'll meet your friend Heinrich—which you do, though you believed him at Trieste—what do you call *that?*'

'It's not uncommon either,' murmured the Swiss and the other three.

'Uncommon!' said the German. 'It's as common as cherries in the Black Forest. It's as common as maccaroni at Naples. And Naples reminds me! When the old Marchesa Senzanima shrieks at a card party on the Chiaja—as I heard and saw her, for it happened in a Bavarian family of mine, and I was overlooking the service that evening—I say, when the old Marchesa starts up at the card-table, white through her rouge, and cries, "My sister in Spain is dead! I felt her cold touch on my back!"—and when that sister *is* dead at the moment—what do you call that?'

'Or when the blood of San Gennaro liquefies at the request of the clergy—the world knows that it does regularly once a-year, in my native city,' said the Neapolitan courier after a pause, with a comical look—'what do you call that?'

'*That!*' cried the German. 'Well! I think I know a name for that.'

'Miracle?' said the Neapolitan, with the same sly face.

The German merely smoked and laughed; and they all smoked and laughed.

'Bah!' said the German, presently. 'I speak of things that really do happen. When I want to see the conjurer, I pay to see a professed one, and have my money's worth. Very strange things do happen without ghosts. Ghosts! Giovanni Baptista, tell your story of the English bride. There's no ghost in that, but something full as strange. Will any man tell me what?'

As there was a silence among them, I glanced around. He whom I took to be Baptista was lighting a fresh cigar. He presently went on to speak. He was a Genoese, as I judged.

'The story of the English bride?' said he. 'Basta! one ought not to call so slight a thing a story. Well, it's

G 2

all one. But it's true. Observe me well, gentlemen, it's true. That which glitters is not always gold; but what I am going to tell is true.'

He repeated this more than once.

Ten years ago I took my credentials to an English gentleman at Long's Hotel, in Bond Street, London, who was about to travel—it might be for one year, it might be for two. He approved of them; likewise of me. He was pleased to make inquiry. The testimony that he received was favourable. He engaged me by the six months, and my entertainment was generous.

He was young, handsome, very happy. He was enamoured of a fair young English lady, with a sufficient fortune, and they were going to be married. It was the wedding trip, in short, that we were going to take. For three months' rest in the hot weather (it was early summer then) he had hired an old palace on the Riviera, at an easy distance from my city, Genoa, on the road to Nice. Did I know that palace? Yes; I told him I knew it well. It was an old palace, with great gardens. It was a little bare, and it was a little dark and gloomy, being close surrounded by trees; but it was spacious, ancient, grand, and on the sea-shore. He said it had been so described to him exactly, and he was well pleased that I knew it. For its being a little bare of furniture, all such places were. For its being a little gloomy, he had hired it principally for the gardens, and he and my mistress would pass the summer weather in their shade.

'So all goes well, Baptista?' said he.

'Indubitably, signore; very well.'

We had a travelling chariot for our journey, newly built for us, and in all respects complete. All we had was complete; we wanted for nothing. The marriage took place. They were happy. *I* was happy, seeing all so bright,

being so well situated, going to my own city, teaching my
language in the rumble to the maid, la bella Carolina, whose
heart was gay with laughter: who was young and rosy.

The time flew. But I observed—listen to this, I pray!
(and here the courier dropped his voice)—I observed my
mistress sometimes brooding in a manner very strange; in
a frightened manner; in an unhappy manner; with a
cloudy, uncertain alarm upon her. I think that I began to
notice this when I was walking up hills by the carriage-side,
and master had gone on in front. At any rate, I remember
that it impressed itself upon my mind one evening in the
South of France, when she called to me to call master back;
and when he came back, and walked for a long way, talking
encouragingly and affectionately to her, with his hand upon
the open window, and hers in it. Now and then he laughed
in a merry way, as if he were bantering her out of something. By-and-by she laughed, and then all went well again.

It was curious. I asked la bella Carolina—the pretty
little one—Was mistress unwell?—No. Out of spirits?—
No. Fearful of bad roads, or brigands?—No. And what
made it more mysterious was, the pretty little one would
not look at me in giving answer, but *would* look at the
view.

But one day she told me the secret.

'If you must know,' said Carolina, 'I find, from what I
have overheard, that mistress is haunted.'

'How haunted?'

'By a dream.'

'What dream?'

'By a dream of a face. For three nights before her
marriage she saw a face in a dream—always the same face,
and only one.'

'A terrible face?'

'No. The face of a dark, remarkable-looking man, in
black, with black hair and a grey moustache—a handsome

man, except for a reserved and secret air. Not a face she ever saw, or at all like a face she ever saw. Doing nothing in the dream but looking at her fixedly, out of darkness.'

'Does the dream come back?'

'Never. The recollection of it is all her trouble.'

'And why does it trouble her?'

Carolina shook her head.

'That's master's question,' said la bella. 'She don't know. She wonders why, herself. But I heard her tell him, only last night, that if she was to find a picture of that face in our Italian house (which she is afraid she will), she did not know how she could ever bear it.'

Upon my word I was fearful after this (said the Genoese courier) of our coming to the old palazzo, lest some such ill-starred picture should happen to be there. I knew there were many there; and, as we got nearer and nearer to the place, I wished the whole gallery in the crater of Vesuvius. To mend the matter, it was a stormy, dismal evening when we, at length, approached that part of the Riviera. It thundered; and the thunder of my city and its environs, rolling among the high hills, is very loud. The lizards ran in and out of the chinks in the broken stone wall of the garden, as if they were frightened; the frogs bubbled and croaked their loudest; the sea-wind moaned, and the wet trees dripped; and the lightning—body of San Lorenzo, how it lightened!

We all know what an old palazzo in or near Genoa is—how time and the sea air have blotted it—how the drapery painted on the outer walls has peeled off in great flakes of plaster—how the lower windows are darkened with rusty bars of iron—how the courtyard is overgrown with grass—how the outer buildings are dilapidated—how the whole pile seems devoted to ruin. Our palazzo was one of the true kind. It had been shut up close for months. Months?—years! It had an earthy smell, like a tomb. The scent of

the orange-trees on the broad back terrace, and of the
lemons ripening on the wall, and of some shrubs that grew
around a broken fountain, had got into the house somehow,
and had never been able to get out again. There it was,
in every room—an aged smell, grown faint with confinement.
It pined in all the cupboards and drawers. In the little
rooms of communication between great rooms it was stifling.
If you turned a picture—to come back to the pictures—
there it still was, clinging to the wall behind the frame,
like a sort of bat.

The lattice-blinds were close shut all over the house.
There were two ugly grey old women in the house, to take
care of it ; one of them with a spindle, who stood winding
and mumbling in the doorway, and who would as soon have
let in the devil as the air. Master, mistress, la bella Carolina, and I went all through the palazzo. I went first,
though I have named myself last, opening the windows and
the lattice-blinds, and shaking down on myself splashes of
rain and scraps of mortar, and now and then a dozing mos-
quito, or a monstrous, fat, blotchy, Genoese spider.

When I had let the evening light into a room, master,
mistress, and la bella Carolina entered. Then, we looked
round at all the pictures, and I went forward again into
another room. Mistress secretly had great fear of meeting
with the likeness of that face—we all had ; but there was
no such thing. The Madonna and Bambino, San Francisco,
San Sebastiano, Venus, Santa Caterina, Angels, Brigands,
Friars, Temples at Sunset, Battles, White Horses, Forests,
Apostles, Doges, all my old acquaintance many times
repeated ?—yes. Dark, handsome man in black, reserved
and secret, with black hair and grey moustache, looking
fixedly at mistress out of darkness ?—no.

At last we got through all the rooms and all the pictures,
and came out into the gardens. They were pretty well
kept, being rented by a gardener, and were large and shady.

In one place there was a rustic theatre, open to the sky; the stage a green slope : the coulisses, three entrances upon a side, sweet-smelling leafy screens. Mistress moved her bright eyes, even there, as if she looked to see the face come in upon the scene : but all was well.

'Now, Clara,' master said, in a low voice, 'you see that it is nothing? You are happy.'

Mistress was much encouraged. She soon accustomed herself to that grim palazzo, and would sing, and play the harp, and copy the old pictures, and stroll with master under the green trees and vines, all day. She was beautiful. He was happy. He would laugh and say to me, mounting his horse for his morning ride before the heat :

'All goes well, Baptista !'

'Yes, signore, thank God ; very well.'

We kept no company. I took la bella to the Duomo and Annunciata, to the Café, to the Opera, to the village Festa, to the Public Garden, to the Day Theatre, to the Marionetti. The pretty little one was charmed with all she saw. She learnt Italian—heavens ! miraculously ! Was mistress quite forgetful of that dream? I asked Carolina sometimes. Nearly, said la bella—almost. It was wearing out.

One day master received a letter, and called me.

'Baptista !'

'Signore.'

'A gentleman who is presented to me will dine here to-day. He is called the Signor Dellombra. Let me dine like a prince.'

It was an odd name. I did not know that name. But there had been many noblemen and gentlemen pursued by Austria on political suspicions lately, and some names had changed. Perhaps this was one. Altro ! Dellombra was as good a name to me as another.

When the Signor Dellombra came to dinner (said the

Genoese courier in the low voice into which he had subsided once before), I showed him into the reception-room, the great sala of the old palazzo. Master received him with cordiality, and presented him to mistress. As she rose her face changed, she gave a cry, and fell upon the marble floor.

Then I turned my head to the Signor Dellombra, and saw that he was dressed in black, and had a reserved and secret air, and was a dark, remarkable-looking man, with black hair and a grey moustache.

Master raised mistress in his arms, and carried her to her own room, where I sent la bella Carolina straight. La bella told me afterwards that mistress was nearly terrified to death, and that she wandered in her mind about her dream, all night.

Master was vexed and anxious—almost angry, and yet full of solicitude. The Signor Dellombra was a courtly gentleman, and spoke with great respect and sympathy of mistress's being so ill. The African wind had been blowing for some days (they had told him at his hotel of the Maltese Cross), and he knew that it was often hurtful. He hoped the beautiful lady would recover soon. He begged permission to retire, and to renew his visit when he should have the happiness of hearing that she was better. Master would not allow of this, and they dined alone.

He withdrew early. Next day he called at the gate, on horseback, to inquire for mistress. He did so two or three times in that week.

What I observed myself, and what la bella Carolina told me, united to explain to me that master had now set his mind on curing mistress of her fanciful terror. He was all kindness, but he was sensible and firm. He reasoned with her, that to encourage such fancies was to invite melancholy, if not madness. That it rested with herself to be herself. That if she once resisted her strange weakness, so successfully as to receive the Signor Dellombra as an English lady would receive any other guest, it was for ever conquered. To make an end, the Signore came again, and mistress received him without marked distress (though with constraint and apprehension still), and the evening passed serenely. Master was so delighted with this change, and so anxious to confirm it, that the Signor Dellombra became a constant guest. He was accomplished in pictures, books, and music; and his society in any grim palazzo would have been welcome.

I used to notice, many times, that mistress was not quite recovered. She would cast down her eyes and droop her head, before the Signor Dellombra, or would look at him with a terrified and fascinated glance, as if his presence had some evil influence or power upon her. Turning from her to him, I used to see him in the shaded gardens, or the large half-lighted sala, looking, as I might say, 'fixedly upon her out of darkness.' But, truly, I had not forgotten la bella Carolina's words describing the face in the dream.

After his second visit I heard master say:

'Now see, my dear Clara, it's over. Dellombra has come and gone, and your apprehension is broken like glass.'

'Will he—will he ever come again?' asked mistress.

'Again? Why, surely, over and over again! Are you cold?' (She shivered.)

'No, dear—but—he terrifies me: are you sure that he need come again?'

'The surer for the question, Clara!' replied master, cheerfully.

But he was very hopeful of her complete recovery now, and grew more and more so every day. She was beautiful. He was happy.

'All goes well, Baptista?' he would say to me again.

'Yes, signore, thank God; very well.'

We were all (said the Genoese courier, constraining himself to speak a little louder)—we were all at Rome for the Carnival. I had been out all day with a Sicilian, a friend of mine, and a courier, who was there with an English family. As I returned at night to our hotel, I met the little Carolina, who never stirred from home alone, running distractedly along the Corso.

'Carolina! What's the matter?'

'O Baptista! Oh, for the Lord's sake! where is my mistress?'

'Mistress, Carolina?'

'Gone since morning—told me, when master went out on his day's journey, not to call her, for she was tired with not resting in the night (having been in pain), and would lie in bed until the evening; then get up refreshed. She is gone!—she is gone! Master has come back, broken down the door, and she is gone! My beautiful, my good, my innocent mistress!'

The pretty little one so cried, and raved, and tore herself, that I could not have held her but for her swooning on my arm as if she had been shot. Master came up—in manner, face, or voice, no more the master that I knew than I was he. He took me (I laid the little one upon her bed in the hotel, and left her with the chamber-women) in a carriage furiously through the darkness, across the desolate Campagna. When it was day, and we stopped at a miserable posthouse, all the horses had been hired twelve hours ago and sent away in different directions. Mark me!—by the Signor Dellombra, who had passed there in a carriage, with a frightened English lady crouching in one corner.

I never heard (said the Genoese courier, drawing a long breath) that she was ever traced beyond that spot. All I know is that she vanished into infamous oblivion, with the dreaded face beside her that she had seen in her dream.

'What do you call *that?*' said the German courier triumphantly: 'ghosts! There are no ghosts *there!* What do you call this that I am going to tell you? Ghosts! There are no ghosts *here!*'

I took an engagement once (pursued the German courier) with an English gentleman, elderly and a bachelor, to travel through my country, my Fatherland. He was a merchant who traded with my country, and knew the language, but who had never been there since he was a boy—as I judge, some sixty years before.

His name was James, and he had a twin-brother John, also a bachelor. Between these brothers there was a great affection. They were in business together, at Goodman's Fields, but they did not live together. Mr. James dwelt in Poland Street, turning out of Oxford Street, London. Mr. John resided by Epping Forest.

Mr. James and I were to start for Germany in about a week. The exact day depended on business. Mr. John came to Poland Street (where I was staying in the house), to pass that week with Mr. James. But, he said to his brother on the second day, 'I don't feel very well, James. There's not much the matter with me; but I think I am a little gouty. I'll go home and put myself under the care of my old housekeeper, who understands my ways. If I get quite better, I'll come back and see you before you go. If I don't feel well enough to resume my visit where I leave it off, why *you* will come and see *me* before you go.' Mr. James, of course, said he would, and they shook hands—both hands, as they always did—and Mr. John ordered out his old-fashioned chariot and rumbled home.

It was on the second night after that—that is to say, the fourth in the week—when I was awoke out of my sound sleep by Mr. James coming into my bedroom in his flannel gown, with a lighted candle. He sat upon the side of my bed, and, looking at me, said:

'Wilhelm, I have reason to think I have got some strange illness upon me.'

I then perceived that there was a very unusual expression in his face.

'Wilhelm,' said he, 'I am not afraid or ashamed to tell you what I might be afraid or ashamed to tell another man. You come from a sensible country, where mysterious things are inquired into, and are not settled to have been weighed and measured—or to have been unweighable and unmeasurable—or in either case to have been completely disposed of, for all time—ever so many years ago. I have just now seen the phantom of my brother.'

I confess (said the German courier) that it gave me a little tingling of the blood to hear it.

'I have just now seen,' Mr. James repeated, looking full at me, that I might see how collected he was, 'the phantom of my brother John. I was sitting up in bed, unable to sleep, when it came into my room, in a white dress, and, regarding me earnestly, passed up to the end of the room, glanced at some papers on my writing-desk, turned, and, still looking earnestly at me as it passed the bed, went out at the door. Now, I am not in the least mad, and am not in the least disposed to invest that phantom with any external existence out of myself. I think it is a warning to me that I am ill; and I think I had better be bled.'

I got out of bed directly (said the German courier) and began to get on my clothes, begging him not to be alarmed, and telling him that I would go myself to the doctor. I was just ready when we heard a loud knocking and ringing at the street door. My room being an attic at the back, and Mr. James's being the second-floor room in the front, we went down to his room, and put up the window, to see what was the matter.

'Is that Mr. James?' said a man below, falling back to the opposite side of the way, to look up.

'It is,' said Mr. James; 'and you are my brother's man, Robert.'

'Yes, sir. I am sorry to say, sir, that Mr. John is ill. He is very bad, sir. It is even feared that he may be lying at the point of death. He wants to see you, sir. I have a chaise here. Pray come to him. Pray lose no time.'

Mr. James and I looked at one another. 'Wilhelm,' said he, 'this is strange. I wish you to come with me!' I helped him to dress, partly there and partly in the chaise; and no grass grew under the horses' iron shoes between Poland Street and the Forest.

Now, mind! (said the German courier). I went with Mr. James into his brother's room, and I saw and heard myself what follows.

His brother lay upon his bed, at the upper end of a long bed-chamber. His old housekeeper was there, and others were there: I think three others were there, if not four, and they had been with him since early in the afternoon. He was in white, like the figure—necessarily so, because he had his night-dress on. He looked like the figure—necessarily so, because he looked earnestly at his brother when he saw him come into the room.

But, when his brother reached the bedside, he slowly raised himself in bed, and looking full upon him, said these words:

'JAMES, YOU HAVE SEEN ME BEFORE TO-NIGHT—AND YOU KNOW IT!'

And so died!

I waited, when the German courier ceased, to hear something said of this strange story. The silence was unbroken.

I looked round, and the five couriers were gone : so noiselessly that the ghostly mountain might have absorbed them into its eternal snows. By this time I was by no means in a mood to sit alone in that awful scene, with the chill air coming solemnly upon me—or, if I may tell the truth, to sit alone anywhere. So I went back into the convent-parlour, and, finding the American gentleman still disposed to relate the biography of the Honourable Ananias Dodger, heard it all out.

LAKE NEMI

By Lord Byron

Lo, Nemi! navelled in the woody hills
So far, that the uprooting wind which tears
The oak from its foundation, and which spills
The ocean o'er its boundary, and bears
Its foam against the skies, reluctant spares
The oval mirrors of thy glassy lake;
And calm as cherished hate, its surface wears
A deep cold settled aspect none can shake,
All coiled into itself and round, as sleeps the snake.

Lake Nemi, the *Lacus Nemorensis* of the ancients, and *Speculum Dianæ* of the poets, evidently occupies the basin of an extinct volcano. It lies at the distance of seventeen miles south-east of Rome. A temple of Diana, mentioned by Strabo, and celebrated throughout all Italy, once stood on its banks. In the years 1885-6 Sir John Lumley (now Lord Savile, K.C.B.), the British Ambassador at Rome, with the permission of Prince Orsini, the owner of the property, caused many excavations to be made on the site of this Artemisium. Among broken columns and other architectural details, votive and culinary utensils in bronze and terra cotta, coins and personal ornaments, a portrait bust

Lake Nemi.

was discovered on a draped plinth, at the base of which was traced the name FUNDILIA RUFA. Recently Lord Savile has presented these classical antiquities to the Nottingham Museum.

It is to this day a place of pilgrimage for visitors in Rome, as it is within a long day's drive.

The engraving is from one of Turner's most lovely drawings. The great master of landscape-painting was evidently inspired by the quiet charm of this lonely lake among the hills, and probably painted it during his second visit to Italy in 1828, when he also painted *Lake Avernus*, which is not many miles distant.

Mr. Cousen's engraving is one of the triumphs of his art. He had previously had much experience in rendering Turner's drawings, but in none of his plates has he ever given us more perfect work.

NARRATIVE OF AN ASCENT OF MONT BLANC IN AUGUST, 1830

BY THE HONOURABLE EDWARD BOOTLE WILBRAHAM

As I was ascending the Mont Anvert on the 1st August, 1830, with Captain Pringle and the Comte de Hohenthal, the beauty of the weather and clearness of the sky put the idea of ascending Mont Blanc into my head. I made a few inquiries of our guide (Dépland), who said there was every probability of the fine weather continuing, and that it would be an excellent opportunity for doing so. He offered willingly to accompany me, but referred me to another guide (Favret), who was ascending the Mont Anvert with a party at the time, and who had been at the top of Mont Blanc already two or three times. I remained in a state of indecision till I reached the Mer de Glace, the first sight of which fixed me in my resolution. I spoke to Favret, who tried to dissuade me from the attempt, but said he would accompany me if I was resolved on making it, and that I should find plenty of guides willing to go with us.

On our way down we met Joseph Marie Coutet, the most experienced of the guides, who had already been at the top of Mont Blanc eight times. He said very bluntly that I had much better not attempt it, and would not even promise his assistance.

On my return to Chamouni I went to old Coutet, the 'Chef des Guides,' who undertook to procure me six guides for my purpose : he also begged permission that his son might accompany us 'en amateur,' which I of course allowed. However, the son never made his appearance.

I ordered the necessary provisions at my inn, and remained quietly at Chamouni for the rest of the day, in order to be as fresh as possible for the morrow.

Six guides at length offered themselves, with whom I was about to close, when the landlord of my inn, the Hôtel de Londres or d'Angleterre, called me aside, and told me that I should run a great risk with these men, if, indeed, they succeeded at all in bringing me to the summit—which I have now no doubt they could not have done—as they had, with the exception of one, never ascended, and that one never by the new road.

After infinite difficulty, however, and long consultations, I engaged six other men—Joseph Marie Coutet, who had reached the summit in the last eight expeditions ; Michel Favret, three times up ; Mathieu Desalloud, never up ; Alexis Devouassoud, two or three times up (these four were regular guides) ; Auguste and Pierre Coutet, cousins ; the first a porter, who had been once up ; the latter, never, and who was to accompany us to the Grands Mulets, and go on with us if it was found necessary to have his assistance.

I found a great reluctance to accompany me on the part of those who had already made the ascent. Coutet, indeed, warned me that I must not rely on the married men making their appearance, and the event proved he was right, as more than one who had promised faithfully the evening before never appeared on the morrow. I afterwards asked one of them (Julien) if he did not regret not having been with me during so prosperous an ascent ; but he told me that he considered his duty towards his wife and family forbad his ever again risking his life for so uncertain a gain. Indeed, he had reason to think so, for he was swept with Coutet into a crevasse by the slip of snow which destroyed three of the guides in the unfortunate expedition of 1820, and was saved by almost a miracle. Out of the forty regularly established guides at Chamouni I could only procure four, with Auguste, a candidate for the situation of guide, and Pierre, the lad, as they called him, though a year older than myself. Having agreed on the sums to be paid them, a further agreement was made (as is always done), that in case we were prevented going any farther than the Grand Plateau only two-thirds were to be paid; and if we only reached the Grands Mulets, half price was all that they expected.

I amused myself that evening with reading Captain Sherwill's account, but found so many horrors in his recital that I soon closed the book. I gave my purse and some papers to my landlord, with instructions what to do with them in case any accident should occur to us, and went to bed in good time.

Favret woke me early next morning in high spirits, for the weather was lovely, and after breakfast I set off on a mule at about half-past six for Coutet's cottage, which is at the foot of the mountain. A great number of travellers were setting off at the same time on different excursions, who all most cordially wished me success. Pringle and Hohenthal took the road to Martigny and the Grand St. Bernard.

When I arrived at Coutet's cottage I put on a broad-brimmed straw hat and blue cloth jacket, and we proceeded on our way. I saw nothing but grave faces around me, and I fear that I must have been the cause of great anxiety to many a friend and relation of those who accompanied me. At the moment, however, I thought little of this, as the only ideas that entered my head were those of success or failure.

Not a cloud was to be seen, and everything seemed in my favour. At the foot of the mountain I found the rest of my guides, with some of their friends, who had volunteered to carry their burdens during the first part of the ascent.

I left Coutet's cottage at about a quarter-past seven, and for two hours I ascended on my mule through a pine-forest by a steep and, in some places, difficult path. I then quitted my mule and proceeded on foot for about half an hour, when we reached the edge of the Glacier des Bossons. Here our friends left us, and each of the guides shouldered his knapsack. Our baggage consisted of the provisions, a linen cloth to serve for our tent, a couple of blankets, some straw, and a hatchet, with some fire-wood. We had each a spiked pole about six feet long; some of the guides had crampons for their feet, but I did not take any, though I afterwards found that they would have assisted me, and should recommend everyone to be provided with them.

We were three hours crossing the glacier, which we did without much difficulty; the surface was rough, and we had to descend into many of the crevasses—which, however, are never there of any great size—in order to pass them. We scrambled about from crag to crag (of ice), and I found myself highly amused at the novelty of the scene. The ice, which at first was almost blackened by the 'moraine,' or rubbish, became purer and more dazzling, and I put on a pair of green spectacles with gauze goggles, which were of the greatest use, as my eyes scarcely suffered at all. The thermometer in the shade was at 13 degrees above freezing-point (Réaumur). We were now on the upper part of the Glacier de Tacconai, which employed us about an hour more, when we at last reached the region of deep and perpetual snow. Here we found ourselves close to the Grands Mulets, our resting-place for the night; though, owing to some crevasses, we were forced to make half-an-hour's détour, and finally arrived there at a quarter-past two, having performed our first day's journey in seven hours from Coutet's cottage—an unusually short time.

The Grands Mulets are a row of pointed rocks, so steep that the snow cannot lie in any depth on them. On the western side is a ledge, which we cleared for our resting-place, of about four feet in breadth, and about a hundred feet above the snow. We placed our poles leaning against the rock, and threw the linen over them as a defence against the night air, though it would not have protected us in the least in any hard weather. There is never any rain at this height.

We changed our clothes, which were wetted through by the snow, and hung them on the rock to dry. We then sat down to our cold dinner, with our legs hanging over the edge of the rock, in high spirits at our hitherto successful journey. We enlivened ourselves afterwards with smoking and singing. Groups of people were assembled on the opposite point of the Breven to watch our arrival, and we had the satisfaction of knowing that many persons were, at that moment, thinking of, and perhaps envying, us.

On the Grands Mulets we found the remains of some fire-wood, two empty bottles, and half a bottle of excellent brandy, which had been left by Mr. Auldjo in 1827. Afterwards, on our return to the Grands Mulets, I ordered the guides to leave a bottle or two of wine for my successor, whoever he may be. The sun was exceedingly hot, and I scrambled into the shade of an opposite point of the rock, where I amused myself by taking sketches of the wonderful scenery around me. On the left, as I faced the summit, were the precipitous crags of the Pic du Midi, on the very highest peaks of which I could distinctly see a large chamois bounding from crag to crag in the most extraordinary manner, as he was alarmed by the shouts which we raised to greet him. From the steep sides of the Pic du Midi the greatest number of avalanches fall, which they did every minute, as the powerful rays of the afternoon sun had loosened the snow. They alighted chiefly in a valley to our left, where we could distinctly trace them, without a shadow of danger to ourselves. They were the first I had seen or heard, and those only who have witnessed them can imagine the effects they produced on my mind. We saw hundreds of them, though I believe that none were considered as particularly fine; but during the night we heard some tremendous ones. There is something very awful in the dead silence that follows the fall of one of these monsters.

On our return from the summit we found that a large avalanche had fallen on the path by which we had passed a few hours before.

We fired a pistol here repeatedly, but failed in producing any remarkably fine echo, owing, I think, chiefly to the badness of our weapon.

The view from the Grands Mulets is very beautiful. At our feet lay the Valley of Chamouni in miniature. Above us rose the majestic summit, the object of all our hopes and desires, while to the right the Dôme du Gouter looked like an enormous mountain of itself. A small part of the Lake of Geneva is visible. Between us and the Dôme du Gouter lay a vast expanse of snow, with nothing to break the uniformity of its surface except the dark blue edges of some of the larger crevasses, which stretched across it as if to forbid our further progress. Except the solitary chamois, no living thing was to be seen, though a few species of birds are sometimes found at this height.

We now lighted a fire to prepare some lemonade for the next day's march. At the foot of the Grands Mulets is a small spring of water—the last supply that we were able to obtain, though this, indeed, could only have proceeded from the melting of the snow.

It would be useless attempting to describe the beauty

of the scene when evening drew near, and the rays of the setting sun rose by degrees to the very tops of the surrounding peaks, dyeing them with the most beautiful tints of purple, which faded by degrees into a most delicate pink, till the grey hue of night crept over the whole. The moon rose in great splendour, and I never shall forget the silent impressiveness of the scene, uninterrupted except by the thunder of the avalanches that fell during the night from the sides of the great Pic du Midi into the valley below. I now turned into the tent, if it may so be called, and lay down with a knapsack for my pillow ; and soon afterwards the guides crept in, and we packed together as well as we could, there being only room for two abreast. A small ledge of rough stones which we had raised was our security against rolling over the precipice, and I should have slept most comfortably had we not been so cramped for room that it was impossible for me to move my legs without kicking the head of the unfortunate man beyond me. As it was, the excitement of the undertaking, the anxiety for the result, and the novelty of the scene combined to keep me awake for some time, and a strange variety of ideas crowded on my mind. It frequently occurred to me how little my friends in England could imagine the sort of resting-place I had chosen for myself that night, and I could not quite banish from my mind the possibility that I might never return to them again, though I did not suffer myself to dwell long on such thoughts as these. The night was not particularly cold, and at last I fell asleep.

At two o'clock the next morning we were aroused, and made hasty preparations for our departure. A few grey clouds were floating about, which the guides considered as rather a good sign. The thermometer was at five above freezing-point (Réaumur). I was dressed as on the preceding day, with the addition of a second shirt, cloth trousers instead of the light ones I had worn, a cotton nightcap under my straw hat, which was tied tightly under my chin, thick fur gloves, and cloth gaiters bound close round my feet with packthread. The temperature was exceedingly variable, as the wind blew along some of the valleys which we entered with great force and coldness, while in others we were sheltered from everything (later in the day) except the powerful rays of the sun, reflected, as they were, on all sides from the surrounding walls of snow. We left most of our baggage at the Mulets, taking only two knapsacks, which the guides carried by turns, containing some provisions, a telescope, and a thermometer. Our provisions consisted of chickens, bread, wine, some very acid lemonade, vinegar, chocolate, and dried plums, which are of great use in allaying thirst when kept in the mouth, as snow is not able to produce that effect. Water would have congealed at this height. We also took some eau de Cologne to relieve the acute headache which generally attacks persons at a great height, and from which I suffered afterwards considerably during the ascent.

We scrambled down the Grands Mulets, and reached the snow, where we fastened ourselves together by twos and threes with ropes round our waists. The four most experienced guides took it by turns to lead, which is the most fatiguing post, as the snow yields more or less to the foot, while we followed in the hardened footsteps of our leader.

We set off at half-past two in silence, for we knew that all our powers and strength would be required before the day was over. The moment I had put my foot on the snow, I felt that my respiration was, to a certain degree, impeded; a sensation which afterwards increased most painfully. We walked, however, slowly, with the intention of reserving our strength as much as possible for the latter part of our ascent. The snow was hard and good, and the 'ponts de neige' over the crevasses were firm. For above an hour, we were working our way under an impending cliff of snow, that looked every moment as if about to detach itself from the great mass and to fall on our heads. The crevasses here are numerous, but not so large as those above the Grand Plateau, which we reached after four hours' hard work.

Generally speaking, only a small portion of the crevasses, that are not of great width, is visible; they are crusted over with frozen snow, and it is here that the utmost experience and skill are required in the guides. In crossing these we always carried our poles at a right angle with the supposed direction of the crevasses, and placed our feet softly on the snow, before we leant forward the weight of our bodies. Some we crossed on our hands and knees, making ourselves as *long* as we possibly could. Over others we sent a guide, well secured by ropes, who, when he had got over, sat down with his heels and pole well planted in the snow, while we followed very *delicately* in his footsteps, holding the rope in one hand. I twice sank above my waist, and several times above my knees, in crossing these places during the descent, when the snow was much softer. One of the men (Alexis, I think) sank rather deep once, and fairly screamed with fright, but scrambled out again before we could even tighten the rope which was fastened round his waist.

The Grand Plateau is a vast amphitheatre of snow, apparently surrounded on three sides by almost perpendicular heights, the fourth side being that by which we ascended. Facing us was a line of small bare rocks, called 'Les Rochers Rouges,' near the foot of which lie, deeply entombed in some crevasse, the bodies of the three unfortunate men who perished in 1820. Here we halted for breakfast, but I had most completely lost my appetite, and it was with the greatest difficulty that I forced myself to eat the wing of a chicken and drink a little wine, as I was assured that if I took nothing I should not have strength to carry me to the summit. I already felt very much fatigued.

Having gladly finished my breakfast, in a few minutes we resumed our route, turning towards the left, and traversing the broad plain of the Grand Plateau till we entered a valley, which soon shut it from our view. This road had been discovered by Coutet at the last ascent but one, being a longer but less dangerous route than the old one, which ascended on the right of the 'Rochers Rouges.'

As we passed near the foot of these rocks, Coutet pointed significantly, and said to me in a low tone, 'Ils sont là.' It was a melancholy recollection, and all the guides seemed to feel deeply the loss of their ill-fated comrades; who will in all probability remain embedded beneath the Grand Plateau till the day of judgment.

The most painful part of our journey had now commenced. The heights we had to climb were generally steep, and it was necessary for the leader to cut steps in the snow with a small hatchet made for the purpose. The valleys were filled with enormous crevasses, which generally crossed them from side to side.

The scenery was of that sublime nature of which a man can have no idea till he has seen it. I never conceived anything so splendid as the interior of some of the crevasses we passed. There were enormous grottoes of brilliant ice, with vaults extending farther than the eye could trace, containing enormous icicles of every possible shape. Some of the edges of the crevasses were worked, as if by the hand of man, in the most beautiful fretwork, with wonderful regularity. Their flooring, if I may so call it, seemed generally firm. As far as I could judge, the depth of many seemed to be between two and three hundred feet. I would have given anything to have descended into one, but it was utterly out of the question, as we had then no time to spare, and on our return the edges of the crevasses would have been too soft to bear our weight ; in addition to which, I doubted exceedingly whether the guides would have had strength enough left to pull me up again—indeed, we had not a sufficient length of rope for such an attempt.

The 'ponts de neige' were generally secure, with the exception of one, which we had some difficulty in passing, and which did not give us very pleasing anticipations for our return, when the little snow that was there would be half melted by the mid-day sun.

We passed it, however, and in about two hours after leaving the Grand Plateau we arrived at a wall of snow, about two hundred feet in height, which we were obliged to climb, and which was very nearly perpendicular. My difficulty of breathing had greatly increased ; I had violent shooting pains through my head ; and my guides already felt the same symptoms, though in a less degree.

We ascended in a zigzag direction, resting every ten minutes for two or three, and turning our faces downwards to breathe more freely, whilst the leader was cutting steps in advance. In these short intervals I frequently fell asleep, while the steepness of the place was so great that I was forced to lean my head against the snow in order to preserve my balance. When I moved, I did so almost mechanically. Both the asthmatic and headachy feelings were much relieved when I remained quiet, but instantly recommenced when in action again. Often did I wish that Mont Blanc had never existed ; but the thought of abandoning my attempt never occurred to me, and I kept my wishes to myself. My guides frequently offered to assist me by pulling at the rope round my waist, but I was anxious to do without help if possible ; and, thanks to the strength of my constitution, I was enabled to succeed. I considered myself most fortunate in escaping the spitting of blood, giddiness, and sickness which persons of weaker lungs often experience when at this height.

In about an hour and a half we reached the 'Petits Mulets,' almost the last points of bare rock which are visible on the mountain, where we rested for five or six minutes. Another hour and a half of steep ascent brought us at last to the summit, on which I stepped without the slightest emotion of pleasure. My ideas were confused from my thorough exhaustion, and after stupidly gazing on the vast scene around me, I sat down on a knapsack and fell asleep with my head on my knees.

After nearly ten minutes they woke me, and I found myself much refreshed. At the same time I woke to a more perfect enjoyment of my new situation; that extreme exhaustion which had overpowered my mind as well as my body had passed away, and I was myself again. It is perfectly useless for me to attempt to describe what I saw: I can only say that it amply repaid me for all the dangers and fatigue I had undergone. France, Italy, Savoy, and Switzerland lay at my feet. The Lake of Geneva and Pays de Vaud seemed quite close to me. Mont Rosa, Milan, and the neighbourhood of Genoa, the town itself being hidden by the heights beyond which it is built. On the north, far beyond the Jura, I saw what may have been Dijon, as it has been before seen, and the weather was perfectly clear. The Valley of Chamouni was under our feet, with the Arve running through it like a thread of silver, and the innumerable peaks of the Alps, all looking like pigmies compared with the giant on which I was standing.

My excessive fatigue caused me to forget two or three things I wished to have done, such as looking for the stars with a telescope, some of which, I believe, may be seen: I could not certainly distinguish them with the naked eye. I forgot, too, to fire a pistol, to hear (if I may say so) it make no noise. I did fire it high up for an echo, and it produced a much weaker report. The sky was an extraordinarily dark blue, almost black.

I did not feel that lightness in treading that is often experienced at that height. I lost all appetite and thirst in ascending, but the latter was very great afterwards. The thermometer was at zero.

The summit appeared to me to be about 120 feet long by fifty broad, of an oval shape, with the corner towards the north-west considerably raised. The shape of the surface, consisting entirely of snow, and subject to great vicissitudes of weather, must be perpetually liable to change.

I may here remark that the upper layers of the snow on the mountain are unlike those which fall on the lower regions, being composed of separate globules, unconnected with each other, except by the cohesion of frost.

We remained on the summit only twenty-five minutes— the longest halt during the day—as we were anxious to avoid passing a second night on the mountain.

My feelings were very different when we began to descend from the perfect apathy and indifference with which I had arrived at the top. The triumph of having succeeded in our attempt, the excitement of the guides, as well as of myself, and the ease in descending compared with the fatigue we had previously felt raised our spirits to the highest pitch, and we set off with shouts of joy.

At a very short distance from the summit a butterfly flew past us: we had neither the power nor the inclination to catch it.[1]

In ascending the snow was hard and good, but by midday the sun had softened it, and in most places we trod knee-deep, which was fatiguing and dangerous, as the 'ponts de neige' over the crevasses were insecure.

The glissades were very amusing. Down an angle of 45 degrees, for instance, we slid on our heels, with the pole

---

[1] Near the top of the Faido, a high mountain by the Pass of St. Gothard, I found part of a swarm of bees lying on the snow, most of them frozen, but some still alive.

behind us in the snow, like a third leg. This requires great practice, and at first I never went more than a few yards without falling, which is an excellent joke in soft snow. At the steeper places we fairly sat down, and, with our poles in the snow behind to guide us, lifted up our heels, and away we went like lightning. We had some excellent races in this manner, and I enjoyed them much. Small crevasses were passed in this way without danger, as the rapidity with which we went prevented our sinking.

The excitement of our enterprise was so great that I can affirm, without any idea of boasting, that I did not during the whole time feel the least degree of fear or even nervousness, though I have frequently since shuddered at the remembrance of some of the places we passed. Once, in the beginning, as I looked down on a steep place from a narrow path, I fancied that I saw the rocks and valley below slowly moving along, but I immediately stood still and looked steadily at them, and never felt giddy afterwards.

Our greatest difficulties at this period of the journey were at that exceedingly steep place I noticed in the ascent, which required the greatest caution, and took us more time in descending than we had been in ascending it. No one, however, made even a false step here. The crevasse which I have before particularly alluded to was crossed after many precautions and without accident. In all probability another week would have melted away the little 'pont' that remained and left the valley perfectly impassable. Had we been unable to cross this on our return, we must either have remained on the mountain and, it is needless to add, have perished, or retraced our steps to near the summit, and descended by the dangerous pass of the 'Rochers Rouges.' I do not think, however, that we should have had strength to re-ascend, especially as the snow was so soft, and we should have been soon overtaken by night and (as the next day proved) a storm. I was not aware of the extent of our danger till we had passed it, when I need not say how grateful we all felt for our safe deliverance. The coolness and intrepidity of my guides were beyond all praise. In descending, I did not feel the slightest difficulty in breathing, and the pains in my head gradually decreased. In some places the wind was high, and the light snow drifted along in sheets when disturbed by our footsteps.

On our return to the Grands Mulets, in three hours and a half, we packed up the baggage we had left there, which, like Æsop's load, had been considerably lightened, and arrived on the glacier, where we halted a few minutes to rest. It was exceedingly hot, and I never suffered so much from thirst as then, which nothing would quench, and which I did not get rid of till I put myself into a hot bath on my return to Chamouni.

At the foot of the mountain I found a mule waiting for me ; and we returned to Chamouni about half-past eight, having been half the time descending that was occupied by the ascent. Though at so late an hour, I found crowds of people waiting to receive me in triumph, as, from Chamouni, they could with telescopes distinctly trace our progress. I did not feel much tired, and was too feverish to sleep well, but the next morning I was exceedingly stiff, and not sorry to remain quiet during most of the day. My face was much swelled and the skin turned black and wrinkled, but after a few days peeled off. My eyes scarcely suffered, and that only for a day or two. Had I not worn green spectacles, I firmly believe I should have been blinded : for nothing can give an idea of the dazzling brilliancy of the snow above, as I found when I now and then for a moment took them off. Two of my guides who had only worn green veils over their faces could scarcely see for a day or two after their descent.

It was amusing to find what a lion I became at Chamouni

during the two days I remained there afterwards. The place was crowded with visitors, and some asked me the most absurd questions imaginable.

I cannot pass over in silence the exceedingly liberal conduct of my host, who, though I was a perfect stranger to him, offered to lend me all the money requisite to pay my guides and other expenses, without even asking for any security, as, having had no previous intention of ascending Mont Blanc, I had not brought enough with me for that purpose. I, however, preferred taking one of the guides with me on my return to Geneva. The reasonable charges and great attentions of my host induce me to recommend him most strongly to those who visit Chamouni.

With regard to this expedition, I cannot do better than repeat Coutet's own words when I first applied to him for his assistance. 'If you succeed, you will think nothing of the fatigue and expense; but if you are compelled by weather or any other circumstance to abandon it, you will be exceedingly sorry that the idea ever entered your head.'

In conclusion: I should most earnestly advise no one to attempt the ascent of Mont Blanc; for though I found myself amply repaid by my success for all my fatigue and troubles, the chances are very great indeed against anyone having again a journey so prosperous in weather and every other respect as mine was. But to anyone who does not care for a rough lodging, I strongly recommend to go to the Grands Mulets, which he may easily do with two or three guides at a trifling expense, pass the night there, and return the following day. I should hardly think it possible to return from the Grands Mulets the same day, but, at all events, the night is the most interesting time of the whole. He will there see enough to give him an idea, though an imperfect one, of the awful scenery which is only to be found above. He will have a splendid view during daylight, and (if he times his visit well) a glorious sunset and moonlight afterwards, and plenty of avalanches during the whole of his stay here. He will experience little danger or fatigue, and, moreover, he will have the distinction of being the first man who ever *willingly* halted at the Grands Mulets or half-way house without the intention of proceeding farther.

HAPPY ANGLERS

By W. M. Thackeray

As on this pictured page I look,
This pretty tale of line and hook,
As though it were a novel-book
    Amuses and engages :
I know them both, the boy and girl,
She is the daughter of the Earl,
The lad (that has his hair in curl),
    My lord the County's page is.

A pleasant place for such a pair !
The fields lie basking in the glare ;
No breath of wind the heavy air
    Of lazy summer quickens.
Hard by you see the castle tall,
The village nestles round the wall ;
As round about the hen, its small
    Young progeny of chickens.

It is too hot to pace the keep ;
To climb the turret is too steep ;
My lord the Earl is dozing deep
    His noonday dinner over ;
The postern-warder is asleep ;
(Perhaps they've bribed him not to peep)
And so from out the gate they creep ;
    And cross the fields of clover.

Their lines into the brook they launch;
He lays his cloak upon a branch,
To guarantee his Lady Blanche
    's delicate complexion:
He takes his rapier from his haunch,
That beardless doughty champion staunch—
He'd drill it through the rival's paunch,
    That questioned his affection!

O heedless pair of sportsmen slack!
You never mark though trout or jack
Or little foolish tickleback
    Your baited snares may capture.
What care has *she* for line and hook?
She turns her back upon the brook,
Upon her lover's eyes to look
    In sentimental rapture.

O loving pair! as thus I gaze
Upon the girl who smiles always,
The little hand that ever plays
    Upon the lover's shoulder;
In looking at your pretty shapes,
A sort of envious wish escapes,
(Such as the Fox had for the Grapes)
    The Poet your beholder.

To be brave, handsome, twenty-two;
With nothing else on earth to do,
But all day long to bill and coo;
    It were a pleasant calling.
And had I such a partner sweet;
A tender heart for mine to beat,
A gentle hand my clasp to meet;—
I'd let the world flow at my feet,
    And never heed its brawling.

AN ADVENTURE IN SPAIN

By J. B.

ON the 9th of July, 1839, as my travelling companion, Don Francisco Fontela, and I were about to enter the *parador* or Venta of Huerta, two leagues on this side of Ariza, we met the Saragossa diligence with only two passengers, the other five having remained behind at Calatayud to recover from the fright caused them by a party of robbers. The carriage bore visible marks of violence, as it was pierced by several bullets. We found upon inquiry that the diligence, after being fired upon by four armed men, had been stopped between El Fresno and the above-mentioned town of Calatayud, and the passengers stripped. This intelligence was by no means agreeable to me; but, as I calculated upon entering Calatayud by daylight, where I might take an escort to Almunia, and thence reach Saragossa without danger, I was not much alarmed. As it may be supposed, this event formed for some time the chief topic of our conversation. We were discoursing upon the chances we had to escape the danger which threatened us, when, just as we were entering the town of Ariza, at about three in the afternoon, we saw from the top of a gentle hill which the carriage was then ascending, four men on horseback galloping towards us, sword in hand. We immediately asked the *mayoral* who they were, and he told us that they were Carlists. At first we did not believe him, and thought he was jesting; but we were soon after convinced of the correctness of his information by the appearance of four grim-looking fellows, wearing the *boina*, or Carlist cap, who surrounded our carriage and bid us to stop, flourishing their swords and vociferating all the time 'Viva Carlos V.,' in which cry, however, we did not fail to join. Upon their inquiring whether we had any arms, and what had become of the *escopitero*, or coach-guard, the conductor answered that the carriage contained no arms whatever, and that it had no *escopitero*. They then ordered the *mayoral* to drive into the village, which he did through such crooked and narrow streets that the coach could hardly get along; the Carlists being all the time engaged in plundering its contents. Once out of the town, we were bid to halt; and the carriage consequently stopped in a field at the foot of the mountains and upon the banks of the Ialon, a small rivulet. The chief of the band then came up, and, bidding us get out of the carriage, asked me who I was, what profession I followed, and what object took me to Saragossa. I told him what my name was, and that I was an *attaché* to the British legation in Madrid, as my passport would show. My travelling companion was next interrogated; but, before he could return any answer, I came forward and said that he was my Spanish servant. Don Francisco was an *intendente* going to Saragossa, and I was afraid that the knowledge of his rank and station might aggravate considerably our situation. The interrogatory being at an end, the Carlist chief ordered us, in a more polite manner than before, to take out all our luggage, as he was going to set fire to the carriage, in compliance with the orders he had received from his superior commander. Having done so, we were directed to sit down at some distance under cover of a wall, whilst the Carlists set fire to the carriage, taking care of the bags containing correspondence with Saragossa, France, &c. The carriage was soon a heap of ashes. Profiting, however, by the short interval which this strange *auto de fé* afforded us, and observing, moreover, that our detainers did not seem to wish to carry things to the last extremity with us, I went up to the chief and asked him to let me go, as he could have no object whatever in detaining me, I being an Englishman by birth, and an *attaché* to the British legation. His answer was that he had orders from his superior, General Balmaseda, to conduct before him all persons of distinction that should happen to fall into his hands; and that it was for him to decide whether I should be allowed to continue my journey or not. I was about to urge my claim with greater authority, when the fear of making matters worse, and of compromising the safety of my travelling companion, who had been intrusted to my care, came suddenly to my mind, and I accordingly decided to wait patiently the result.

Meanwhile, another party of Carlists were lying in ambush near the town of Ariza, ready to pounce upon the diligence coming from Saragossa to Madrid, which was expected to pass by at that hour, but, fortunately for the passengers, the post-master of Ariza, who had the good luck to escape detention, rode up to them and warned them of the threatening danger. The diligence, therefore, stopped on the road, and the Carlists were disappointed of their prey. A *galera*, or waggon, belonging to a certain carrier of Saragossa, named Garcia, happening to pass at this time through Ariza, was stopped by the same band which attacked us. This vehicle contained, if I recollect right, eight passengers going to France. These were, a lieutenant of the foreign legion in the service of Spain, a fencing-master, and a baker, all Frenchmen; a copper-smith, a cooper, a barber from Saragossa, and lastly, a lieutenant of artillery of the *milicia nacional*, who was going to Teruel, where he held a public situation; besides two women, with whom the Carlists did not in the least interfere. All the other passengers, with the exception of the French lieutenant, who, after being stripped of all his money and valuables, contrived to escape, were marched to the spot where my friend and I were sitting, and their trunks and other luggage came to increase the booty made upon a previous occasion. Orders were likewise given to fire the waggon; but, it being quite impossible that its huge mass should pass through the narrow streets of the town, and, moreover, as there was a danger that the flames might communicate to the adjoining houses, the order was countermanded, and the carrier suffered to redeem his waggon, mules, and cargo, not belonging to the passengers, for the comparatively small sum of three thousand reals, or about thirty pounds English money. The waggon was chiefly loaded with wool, which the carrier was also allowed to keep upon his declaring that it belonged to him.

Some hours had passed in questioning the passengers who had come by the waggon, and separating their luggage from what constituted the load of the waggon, when, at about six o'clock in the afternoon, we were told to prepare to march. We were all provided with donkeys to ride, and I must, in justice, say that the captain gave me the best beast and told the driver to take every care of me. My friend rode the same horse which had belonged to the postillion of the mail, and, after great trouble and considerable loss of time, we started on our expedition. Our order of march was as follows—my travelling companion and I were in front of the column; next came the *mayoral* and *zagal* of the mail, and the mules belonging thereto; the passengers of the *galera* followed; lastly, the line of march was closed by several mules or donkeys carrying the luggage or goods captured upon the two occasions. This long convoy was escorted by two lancers only: one of them, named Garcia, was a sergeant of whom I shall have occasion to speak hereafter. The other was a coarse and brutal fellow, the servant of an officer belonging to another troop.

When I saw that we were so slightly guarded, and that, besides ourselves, we had in our favour the drivers of the mules, who had been reluctantly dragged away from home on this service, I began to consider how shameful it was that so many men should be led to captivity, and perhaps to death, by only two men on horseback, and how easy it would be to regain our liberty. I communicated my project to some of my fellow-sufferers, but nowhere did I find the aid which I expected. The fencing-master only said to me in French, 'Il n'y a pas d'union entre nous ; sans cela je suis sûr de mon homme.'[1] Time passed in this and other conversation, and, at nine in the afternoon, we arrived at the *corral*, or breeding-yard, of *cabra la fuente*, three leagues from Ariza, where Sergeant Garcia bade us enter one by one, and shut us in, placing one of the drivers at the door, in order that none should escape. The frequent conversations in French which he had overheard without being able to understand, the discontent which he read in our countenances ; and last, not least, the gesticulations and threatening mien of the French fencing-master, raised his suspicions, and he thought proper to confine us in a place of safety. I spread my cloak on the ground and lay down on it, much less with an intention to sleep, for I was certain not to close my eyelids, than to rest my worn-out limbs ; I also waited anxiously for the arrival of Captain Arranz, who was in command of this force and who was expected every moment, as I wished to speak to him about my liberation. He came at last, at about twelve o'clock, and I prepared to express my sentiments to him in the best manner I could. But, before I ventured to do so, I inquired from one of the soldiers what were the real character and intentions of that individual, and what the object of the incursion he was then making. I was told that he was a very good sort of

---

[1] We are not united, otherwise I should be sure of my man.

fellow, and that he was assisted in the execution of his orders by a certain Carlist clergyman, who exercised great influence over him. Having asked to see the curate, he was pointed out to me, and I immediately went up to him with a view of gaining him to my cause. Strange to say, no sooner had I addressed him than he recognised me by the sound of my voice, it being then pitch dark, as we were not allowed to have a light in the place, and addressed me by name. I then found out that he was no other than the curate of Alhama, whom I had known upon a former occasion. He had gone over to the Carlists, and, profiting now by the incursion made into Aragon, had accompanied them with a view of settling some family affairs and getting a bill cashed at Ariza. I immediately explained my case to him, and begged that he should use his influence with the captain to obtain my liberation and that of my servant. He did so, but to no effect; for shortly after the captain himself came up to me, and said he was very sorry not to be able to accede to my wishes. Had he been present at the time of my being taken, it might have been accomplished; but now it was impossible, for, were he to let me go, some of his soldiers would undoubtedly denounce his act to Balmaseda, who would have him cashiered or perhaps put to death for daring to disobey his orders. He, however, promised that I should be treated with every possible regard and attention; that I would have the best horse to ride and every comfort that could be procured on the road. Seeing that all my arguments were in vain, and that I could not prevail upon the captain to set me at liberty, I resigned myself to my fate, and decided to wait the course of events. Captain de Joaquin Arranz, better known by the surname of Joaquinillo, which his own men gave him, was a middle-aged, common-looking man, who, having embraced the party of Don Carlos, and joined the rebels in Aragon, had risen from the ranks, and obtained promotion by his fidelity and his courage. He was a good-natured and kind-hearted man.

We started at two in the morning, with a most piercing cold. I rode by the side of the curate, all the time keeping my eye upon the mule that carried my luggage and that of my friend. In this way we trudged along for some time, until the cold of the morning began to increase in such a manner that I do not recollect having ever felt anything like it. I had on a pair of summer trousers, so that, although I wrapped myself up in my cloak as well as I could, I was literally frozen. This, coupled with mental anxiety, and the reflection of the impression which the news of my capture might make on my family and friends at Madrid, brought on an illness from which I suffered greatly.

At about five o'clock P.M. we passed by the town of * * * *, which is very agreeably situated in the middle of a well-cultivated plain. Here the curate left us in search of some men whom he had sent forward to cash a bill; and we continued our march till seven, when we were ordered to halt. This order was a godsend for me, for I was so tired that I could hardly move. I wrapped myself up in my cloak, and threw myself on the ground. After one hour's sleep, which refreshed me considerably, I awoke and found that the curate was not yet returned from his expedition; and I began to fear that I had lost a friend, and that, perhaps, he would never come back. At nine o'clock we resumed our march, until we arrived at Milmarcos, seven hours distant from the breeding-yard where we had passed the night. Here I had the consolation to see again the curate, who joined us on the road. He told us that he had lost his way, and had been obliged to take a guide.

Milmarcos is the last town of Castile on the frontier of Aragon. Upon our arrival there, my friend the curate took me with him to the house of the curate of the village, where breakfast was served. I could hardly swallow a cup of chocolate which was offered to me; but my protector remained in the house partaking of a tolerably good breakfast in company with the chief of our escort and the rest of the prisoners. Finding myself alone and unobserved, I took the opportunity of tearing the posting-licence which I had with me, as it contained a note stating that I was the bearer of despatches from the English legation at Madrid. I was afraid that, were this circumstance to be found out, I might be asked to give them up. I tore, likewise, all the letters of introduction for Calatayud and Saragossa, of which I was the bearer, and wherein the object of my journey to the latter place was mentioned.

At Milmarcos, the chief of our escort released the *bagajeros* (mule-drivers) and their beasts, and took fresh ones. He also set at liberty the conductor and postillion of the mail, moved, no doubt, by a laudable sentiment of generosity. He sold a good portion of the pork taken in the waggon, at about eight shillings per *arroba*, or twenty-five pounds weight, and divided the produce among his own men, each having for his share twenty-six reals.

The party consisted of seven men, one sergeant, and the chief, who had the rank of captain. They were all mounted, and armed with lances. Each of them had a nickname, or war-cry, by which he was known, the simple enumeration of which will convey a sufficient idea of what sort of people they were. *Matauras*, or priest-killer, was the name of one, and it appears he had come by that appellation from his having once assassinated a venerable priest at Siguenza. *Iuanon*, *Fisonomia*, were the names of two of the others; the latter was a ruffian, who might have cut a gallant figure even among Palillo's band of assassins. *Burguillos* was the nickname of a fourth, who boasted of having killed with his own hand no less than twenty-two individuals, without the least provocation on their part; there was another one named *Cebada*, or barley. Garcia was the name of the sergeant, and I shall only say this about him, that a few days before our capture he had received five hundred lashes by order of Balmaseda.

With such an agreeable company we set out for the third time, and marched in the direction of *El Molino de la Decheso*. As we trudged along the road, seeing myself alone with the curate and one of the drivers, a trusty man named Pascual Mañaco, I made a last effort to obtain my liberty, through the intercession of the former. I began by making him observe that the chief of the party had allowed the conductor and postillion of the mail to escape while he kept me still in his power, exposing me to the great injury which both my health and my affairs would sustain by keeping me so long, and exposing me to so many hardships and privations. I protested that I had nothing to fear from Balmaseda, were I to be conducted to his presence ; and that he would, no doubt, release me immediately. These arguments seemed to have some weight upon the curate. He kindly promised me to renew his application at the first halting, and I bound myself, if I obtained my liberty, to bestow upon the soldiers four gold doubloons which I had by me, and, besides, to pay handsomely the driver who would undertake to accompany me to Saragossa. In order, however, to make things still more satisfactory, and in order to give the curate a proof of my gratitude, I took my gold watch, and, presenting it to him, begged him to keep it in token of remembrance. The curate refused at first ; but upon my insisting, he accepted my present and thanked me for it. This gave me courage, and, not doubting that I might already consider myself as free, I went up in great spirit and told Don Francisco to keep himself and horse in readiness, as I had no doubt that we should be set free almost immediately.

At about noon we arrived at *El Molino* (the mill), where

we halted. Sentries were placed all round it to prevent our escape, but we were otherwise allowed the full range of the building. Don Francisco and I stretched ourselves on the floor, as we were exceedingly tired. We were soon roused by the sound of a drum, and, looking out, we saw a party of men advancing upon the mill. These proved to be a party of infantry, about forty in number, with some cavalry officers, all belonging to the Carlist division commanded by a partizan chief named Miguel. The chiefs of both parties shook hands together, and joined in one of the rooms, whilst the soldiers went about the place. Don Francisco and I were admitted into their circle, and remained with them until the dinner-hour. The newspapers found in the mail-bags were produced, and the curate began to read them to the company, of whom few, if any, were able to read. Strange enough, the papers happened to contain some letters from Cabrera and Arias Tejiero to Don Carlos, which, having been intercepted, were published by order of the Government. The correspondence turned, as it is well known, upon the relative position of the Carlist troops and officers in Aragon, and those which still supported the cause of Don Carlos in the Basque provinces.

But I will not pass without notice a fact highly creditable to these people, and which marks the natural courtesy of the Spaniards. Though we were surrounded by people professing different opinions, and following a course widely different from our own, men who would not have scrupled to put us to death; although the curate now and then read to them paragraphs highly irritating and injurious, inasmuch as they treated their sovereign with the greatest contempt, and cast ridicule upon their generals, not a word was uttered calculated to wound our feelings as partizans of Queen Isabella.

It was not till four o'clock in the afternoon that the worthy curate had an opportunity to enter into negotiation with the chief of our escort, in order to obtain my liberation and that of my travelling companion. He took him apart and spoke to him for some time. The result of the conference, however, was not so satisfactory as I had anticipated. Joaquinillo's answer was that he could not decide without consulting his men, since, were he to grant my request, they might afterwards inform against him. I myself went up to him in order to vanquish his scruples, and offered to go and treat with the lads, promising at the same time that if the negotiation were successful, I would remit him twenty pounds sterling, upon my arrival at Calatayud, besides the four gold doubloons which I had engaged to give to his men. He assured me that I had nothing to fear, and I would shortly be set free, as he had no doubt that his men would accede to my proposition. Whilst the negotiation was going on, the curate thought proper to acquaint Miguel, the chief lately arrived, of what was passing, and, as the latter was the curate's friend, he not only approved of the step, but came good-naturedly to congratulate me upon my approaching liberation. A passport was immediately prepared for me and my servant, Don Francisco, which I happened to take to Joaquinillo to have his signature. What was my astonishment to find that he refused to sign it, upon the plea that his men, at the instigation of Sergeant Burguillos, would not consent to my liberation! This ruffian had lately made himself guilty of every cruelty and excess, committing various robberies and extorting money even from people devoted to Don Carlos. Finding that I had offered money for my liberation, he fancied that I was a person of importance and had large sums with me, and that my being taken to the Carlist camp might be looked upon as an eminent service, and as a sort of atonement for the crimes of which he had made himself guilty. I went up to him and made use of every entreaty, but in vain; he constantly refused to be a party to my liberation.

Cruelly disappointed in my expectation, I again fell into a desponding state of mind, the more so that I soon learned that the cooper, the copper-smith, and the French baker had been suffered to depart for no other reason than their being poor. We were soon ordered to march, and took the road to Odon, Miguel and his men marching in an opposite direction towards Castile. Soon after our departure a violent dispute arose between Sergeant Burguillos and Joaquinillo, the former accusing the latter of having received money for the liberation of his prisoners. Incensed at this, Joaquinillo ordered three of his men to gallop after the poor men, but although they found them at a short distance from the place, they contented themselves with taking everything from them, and suffered them to continue their journey, saying, on their return, that they had not found them. Far from putting an end to the dispute, this incident aggravated it, and, as we went along, there was nothing but vociferation and abuse, the men taking the part of one or other of their officers, until I began to fear an explosion, of which we all might be the victims.

At about one we arrived at a village between *El Molino* and Odon, the name of which has escaped my memory; our party being diminished by five persons, besides some of the mule-drivers, who, being no longer wanted, had been suffered to depart. I threw myself on the ground; but I was soon roused from my slumber by one of the men belonging to the escort, who most unceremoniously kicked at me, saying that he wished to say a few words. This man was a spare, thin, savage-looking fellow, with small piercing eyes; Cebada (barley) was his name. He came to tell me that one of his comrades had just been talking of asking me for one doubloon, and that unless I immediately gave it up, he apprehended there would be a row. I thanked him for the information, but refused giving the money, upon the plea that, not knowing how long I might be kept a prisoner, I did not like to part with my money; but if he and his comrades could agree to let me go, I would willingly give up to them every farthing I had about me. Whilst I was talking to this man, the signal for mounting was given, and I lost the last hope of accomplishing my liberation. We then started, bound for Odon, the small town before mentioned.

During the night some of the ruffians who composed our escort, taking advantage of the obscurity, went up to one of the muleteers, and threatening him with instant death if he uttered a word, stopped the luggage mule confided to his care, broke open a trunk, the contents of which they proceeded to divide among themselves. Information of this outrage soon reached the ears of their commander, Joaquinillo, who, blind with rage, rode up to the men, and threatened to inform against them upon his arrival at general quarters.

It was night when we reached Odon, where we were to spend a few hours. In order to avoid a repetition of what had just occurred, I directed Pascual, my muleteer, a fine, active lad, of about eighteen, to look out for a safe place for himself and the mule that carried my luggage. I, followed by Don Francisco, went to the house of the curate of the village, where I fixed my quarters. After taking some refreshment, I laid down and went to sleep; but I had scarcely shut my eyes when I was suddenly awakened by a great noise in the street. I looked out, and saw Joaquinillo in the act of beating two men, one of whom belonged to his own party, whilst the other, who was a friend of Burguillos, had deserted his company at *El Molino*, and joined us. Fearing lest all these broils and disputes should bring on something very unpleasant for us prisoners, I made a last effort, if not to obtain my liberation and that of my travelling companion, at least to part company with a set of ruffians over whom it now became quite clear that their

K

captain had but little command. As the town of Molina, where General Balmaseda had his headquarters, was only four leagues distant from Odon, I proposed to Joaquinillo that he should allow me to remain at the curate's house, whilst he and his men marched to that place, and ascertained what were the general's intentions respecting us, engaging my solemn word not to depart from the village until Balmaseda's wish was known. All my arguments, however, were in vain. Joaquinillo pulled out his instructions and gave them to me to read. The order was thus conceived :—' The Captain, Lieutenant-Colonel by brevet Don Joaquin Arranz, shall repair to the road between Saragossa and Madrid, shall stop the mail which is to leave Madrid on the 8th, besides all the diligences and other carriages that may happen to pass by, and will bring before me everything he may find on them, and all the passengers of distinction. He will likewise go down Alhama, and will seize all persons attending the baths there, and lead them before my presence, excepting those that may be so ill that their lives might be endangered through it.' Having read the instructions, I gave him back the paper, and suggested to him that my health being considerably shaken by the fatigues of the journey, which I could no longer endure, I was naturally comprised in the number of those who were not to be marched to the general quarters of Balmaseda ; to which he replied that the order alluded merely to the people apprehended at the baths of Alhama, and by no means to those arrested on the road, and he ended by observing that in the state of insubordination in which his men were, he dare not take upon himself the responsibility of setting me at liberty, since, were he to do so, his life and that of the curate were in great danger among such a set of ruffians.

Seeing all hope vanish before me, I resigned myself to my fate, and prepared to start. We started at about ten, towards the river Celta ; but we had scarcely marched half an hour, being then in a plain, two miles distant from Odon, when our attention was attracted by a great noise in the rear of our column. It was Joaquinillo, who was disputing with some of his men, and threatening them with a severe castigation as soon as he reached general quarters. The vociferation increased, the dispute rose high, and I expected at every moment to see them lay hands on their commander. It happened as I had foreseen ; Sergeant Garcia, who rode on the right of Joaquinillo, suddenly pounced upon him, snatched his sabre from him, and aimed a terrific blow at his head, which the other parried with his arm. At the same time he hallooed to the men in front of the column to come to his assistance. ' Cebada !' he said ; ' now is the time ; go it boys, and we shall soon see who commands here !' Mad with rage, Joaquinillo begged Burguillos to lend him his sabre that he might punish the insolence of Garcia ; but that wretch, who was in the plot, rode away, leaving his captain to get out of the scrape as well as he could. Garcia then approached Joaquinillo, obliged him to dismount, which being done, our boxes and trunks were laid on the ground, broken open with the point of their lances, and their contents shared among them. Among the trunks, that of the French fencing-master was conspicuous, since, besides a quantity of beautiful arms, such as swords, sabres, pistols, and so forth, it contained about one hundred pounds in money, the whole of which the ruffians proceeded to divide among themselves, notwithstanding the prayers and entreaties of their own captain and of the worthy curate. The Frenchman's rage when he saw his doubloons pass into the hands of these men cannot well be described. He pulled his hair, stamped his foot, and cried like a child, saying that he was a ruined man, and that he had lost in one unlucky hour the savings of many years. For my part, I own that, when I saw such a scene of confusion and want of discipline, I began to fear the worst consequences, and, therefore, taking with me my muleteer, Pascual, I went up to the curate, who, with his two servants, Thomas and Andrew, was standing aloof from the party. My comrade, Francisco, being in as great a state of alarm as myself, came also there for protection, and joined our party. Meanwhile, the men, after holding a short conference, despatched one of their number to me. It was Cebada, and I saw him approach us with a countenance which boded no good. Taking me apart, as well as the curate, he asked me what money I had. I answered him that I had no more than the four doubloons which I had in the first instance offered as the price of my liberation; these he made me give him, adding that I now might go with my servant whither I pleased. Shortly after Sergeant Garcia made his appearance, and, mixing in the conversation, asked me what I had done with my watch. I told him that, having experienced much kindness at the hands of the curate during our march, I had thought it proper to present him with it, in token of gratitude; upon which he went up to the curate, and asked him to surrender it, which he did. Thus ended this scandalous scene; the insurgents, seven in number, then left us, taking with them the horse belonging to the captain, who remained on foot.

I might easily have profited by the opportunity which now presented itself, to part company with these people; but, not knowing to what dangers I might be exposed on the road, I preferred remaining with the captain, and waiting for a more favourable opportunity. I ought here to observe that, owing to some circumstance for which I cannot well account, my portmanteau was not touched by the insurgents.

Having replaced on the mules' backs those articles of our luggage which they would not take away, we resumed our march in the direction of Corija del Campo. One hour afterwards we halted at a place distant two leagues from the above-mentioned town, where a scene awaited us far more tragic than the one which we had just witnessed. The sun was high and the heat was insufferable. Our first step after halting was to run to a neighbouring fountain to quench the raging thirst which devoured us. The French fencing-master, always the first on such occasions, seized a large pitcher which happened to be there, drank a copious draught, and passed it over to the curate, who drank, and gave it to me. I then returned it to the Frenchman, who offered it to Burguillos, who had by that time approached the fountain on horseback. I was looking in another direction, when I heard all of a sudden a most terrific shriek. I looked, and saw Burguillos stretched on the ground with one hand on his head, screaming at the top of his voice that he had been murdered; and saw, almost at the same time, the fencing-master intrepidly attacking Joaquinillo, sword in hand. Without ascertaining the cause of the disturbance, and thinking, no doubt, that a party of the enemy had suddenly made its appearance upon the spot, the curate, in great fright, galloped off. I followed him on foot, entreating him to stop and allow me to mount behind him; but this he would not allow, on the plea that if we were to fall in with a party of Christinos they would do me no harm, whilst they would most undoubtedly put him to death. I then left him, and perceiving a stone wall at some distance from the road, hid myself behind, to wait the result of this most unexpected occurrence, which I could nowise explain. I afterwards ascertained that, whilst Burguillos was in the act of raising the pitcher which the fencing-master tendered him to his mouth, the latter stabbed him twice with a dagger which he had concealed in his coat-sleeve; taking then the sabre of his adversary, who lay stretched on the ground, he went up to attack Joaquinillo, repeating all the time, with theatrical emphasis, 'Stand by my side, national guards! Liberty for ever!' At this moment one of the muleteers took up a stone, and hurled it with such dexterity and violence at the poor Frenchman's head that it struck him on the right temple and brought him senseless to the ground, and Joaquinillo coming up soon ran his sabre through his body. Such was the end of this madman, who, when his assistance might have been of some use, had rejected my proposition to attack the escort; and who, goaded now to revenge by the loss of his savings, made a useless display of courage, and brought death on himself.

I had been about an hour in my hiding-place, when I again saw our column moving slowly along the road. I confess that I was long hesitating whether I should join them or not, as I might easily have procured a guide to take me to Calatayud; but the intendente was still among them, and as he had been strongly recommended to my care, I did not like to abandon him, the more so that, had he reached general quarters without me, and had his real name been ascertained, he would have been put to death immediately. I therefore joined the column, determined to share my comrade's fate or save his life. Soon after Burguillos made his appearance under the care of one of the passengers of the galera. He was badly, though not mortally, wounded; but he was so weak from the loss of blood that he was obliged to remain at a village one league on this side of Corija, where we made a short stay.

As we were approaching the river Celta our small escort began to give visible signs of fear, as we were then getting near to a district which was in the possession of the Queen's troops. We passed through Corija without stopping, and, having crossed the river, found ourselves on the road which goes from Saragossa to Ceruel. Here, Joaquinillo, having seen in the distance a picquet of cavalry,

LEANING TOWER OF SARAGOSSA.

By David Roberts, R.A.

thought they were Christinos, and galloped away in an opposite direction, obliging us to follow him. Having, however, found out that the suspicious horsemen belonged to their own party, he drew up, and we then proceeded at a moderate rate till we came to the foot of a mountain-chain in those districts, which the Carlists emphatically called their line, and which afforded them great protection, being generally very high and of difficult access. We entered these mountains through a narrow and precipitous pass, about two miles long, at the end of which we met a few sheep grazing, the first that I had seen during my peregrination. Here we halted for a while, and after some time resumed our march. When we were about to start, we found that one of our fellow-prisoners, the passenger by the waggon, had disappeared. He was an artillery officer, and fearing that upon his arrival at general quarters he would be immediately shot, he took advantage of the halt we made at this spot to make his escape from his guards. The poor man, however, chose a most unlucky moment; for, scarcely had he proceeded half a mile on his road when he was stopped by a cavalry soldier, who presented him to the commander of our escort, just at the time we were entering the town of Rubielos. The soldier stated that he had found the man alone on the road, who told him that he was a Carlist artillery soldier belonging to the garrison at Segura; but that, suspecting all was not right with him, he had brought him to his presence. Hearing this, Joaquinillo got into a great rage, saying, 'The scoundrel lies: he is no Carlist, he is one of our prisoners just escaped from us;' then, turning towards his men, he made them a signal, and told them to take away the guilty officer. Suspecting some mishap, I went up to Joaquinillo, and earnestly inquired of him what orders he had given respecting the prisoner, when he answered me with the greatest composure, 'I have ordered him to be shot!'

At about eight in the morning of the 12th we started for Pancrudo, a small town situated in the midst of mountains, where we arrived at one o'clock, and found that Brigadier-General Rolo, the brother-in-law of Cabrera, had just left the place at the head of two battalions and two troops of cavalry, in the direction of Lucena, owing to which no provisions of any sort could be found in the place. I made every effort to procure eggs, but none were to be found. The only food we could obtain was dried cod-fish, cooked with rancid oil, and smelling of garlic, of which, of course, I was obliged to partake with the rest, to escape starvation. As we were sitting at this luxuriant repast, in came galloping an orderly of Balmaseda, who brought a verbal message from that chief to Joaquinillo. Taking him apart, he communicated to him the orders of which he was the bearer, whilst the curate and myself remained in suspense, not knowing what to think. Presently Joaquinillo made a sign to me and to the curate to approach, and told us that he had received orders from the General to proceed forthwith to a place called Martin del Rio, with all his prisoners, enjoining him at the same time to treat me with every consideration and respect. It is impossible for me to describe the effect which these words of peace had upon me; they were like the balm poured upon the wounds—like the return of fine weather after a tempest.

About sunset of the same day we came in sight of the town. We were at about a musket-shot from it, when we saw four men on horseback making for our party. One of them, who came in the middle, and who was taller and stouter than the rest, rode with an air of great authority, which called my attention. This made me inquire of the curate and Joaquinillo, who rode by my side, who could these be; when to my great astonishment I heard them say to each other—'It is General Balmaseda!' We immediately dismounted, seeing which, the General came up, gave

me his hand, and, addressing me in English, asked me
whether I could speak Spanish. I answered him in the
affirmative, telling him at the same time that I was
delighted to hear him speak my native tongue, in which,
however, he never uttered another word. I took hold of
his arm, which he offered me, and we walked towards the
village, followed at some distance by the curate, Joaquinillo, and the General's own escort. Upon arriving at his
quarters the General ordered the prisoners to be billeted
about the town and the luggage and goods removed to his
own house, desiring me and my friend to take up our
residence there, adding, with much courtesy and affability,
'I am exceedingly sorry that my people have caused you
such delay and inconvenience; but, on the other hand, this
affords me the pleasure of having you in my company and
giving you an opportunity of judging by yourselves whether
a Carlist chief can always be made responsible for the
excesses committed by his subordinates.' He then asked
me whether I had any complaint to make against Joaquinillo or his men. I told him I had none, and that, although
I had been exceedingly annoyed by being taken so far out
of my way, I was yet disposed to forgive him, in consideration for the kind treatment which I now experienced at his
hands; and I concluded by advising him to give strict
orders in future that the chiefs of such marauding expeditions should not interfere with foreigners or gentlemen
belonging to foreign legations. He offered me his excuses,
saying that, although he had fully intended to do so, in the
present case he had forgotten to give the order.

After a short delay, during which time the attaché and
his friend were treated with every kindness, Balmaseda
gave them money and an escort and allowed them to depart; and, after a few days' journey, they found themselves
safe among their friends at Saragossa.

THE NUPTIALS OF THE DOGE OF VENICE WITH THE ADRIATIC SEA

By Lord Morpeth

DOGE

Thou blue and buoyant wave,
    That lav'st my ducal tower,
Whom nature to me gave
    For pastime and for power,
I ride upon thy foam,
    I revel by thy side,
I claim thee as my home,
    I woo thee for my bride.

ADRIATIC

Lord of the glitt'ring town,
    The vineyard and the lea,
The mountain and the down,
    What would'st thou on the sea?
Thy mandates cannot sway
    My waters as they roll;
My wild waves in their play
    Will spurn at thy control.

Woodbury-Gravure.

THE DUCAL PALACE, VENICE.

By Samuel Prout.

DOGE

The portion of my hand
   No monarch ever bore,
A gift from ev'ry land,
   A spoil from ev'ry shore;
Lo! Venice is thine own,
   Her beauty and her might,
The lions of her throne,
   The bowers of her delight—

Her massive domes and halls,
   Her pillar'd corridors,
Her painting-cover'd walls,
   Her marble-chequer'd floors;
The portico and shrine,
   The arsenal and quay,
Fair daughter of the brine,
   I give them all to thee.

ADRIATIC

I bathe Gargano's steep,
   Otranto's castled tower,
Ravenna's mould'ring keep,
   Ancona's Doric bower;
But, Venice, on my strand
   I see not aught like thee;
Then, first upon the land,
   Be first upon the sea.

Ev'ry gem of the wave
    Shall deck the spouse I wed,
Of my pearl-lighted cave,
    My coral-pillow'd bed ;
All precious things that grow
    Beneath the amber shower,
A thousand fathom low,
    Shall be the sea-maid's dower.

DOGE

I pledge to thee my vow,
    Long as my ruling star
Binds commerce to my prow,
    And conquest to my car :
Each accurs'd Moslem slave
    From thy waters shall flee ;
None may tread on thy wave,
    But the Faithful and Free.

ADRIATIC

Thy fleets where'er they sail,
    For glory or for gain,
Through sunshine and through gale,
    I'll speed across the main ;
The thunder of my deep
    Shall rescue thee from harm,
I'll shed, too, round thy sleep
    The music of my calm.

DOGE

Uplift the streamer bright,
   Upraise the golden spear,
Each armour-girded knight,
   Each gay-clad gondolier;
A thousand voices sing,
   As in thine azure tide
I drop the mystic ring,
   My Adriatic bride.

ADRIATIC

Strike your ocean-tun'd shell,
   Sister-choirs of the deep,
In your emerald cell
   Lofty festival keep:
Chief of the countless gold!
   Chief of the fearless sword!
The nuptial rite is told,
   I take thee for my lord.

ORIENTAL SPORTS

By the Rev. Hobart Caunter, B.D.

All Mohammedan sovereigns in India, whether dependent or supreme, from the time of Akbur to the present, have evinced a decided partiality for those exhibitions in which that celebrated monarch took such delight; and the elephant fights of Lucknow have been notorious ever since the Mohammedan princes first established their courts in that city. Whenever the king of Oude is visited by any European of note, he always has an elephant fight by way of entertaining his guests.[1]

The manner of conducting these sports is as follows:—A female elephant is introduced and led to the centre of the enclosure, where she stands upon a gentle elevation, looking around her with an evident consciousness of what is about to take place. The two male combatants are now driven in at different entrances.

The bodies of these pampered animals are covered with a strong rope netting, to which the mahoots cling during the shock of contention; and this is frequently so violent as to dislodge them in spite of their utmost efforts to prevent such an issue, exposing them to imminent peril—indeed, those unfortunate persons are occasionally trodden to death by the angry elephants when thrown from their necks or haunches. Sometimes they are struck down by the trunks of the enraged animals whilst encouraging or goading them to the combat: they, however, generally con-

[1] Written in 1837.

trive to evade such disasters, by retreating towards the tails of their respective charges, as these latter meet in full encounter.

So soon as the huge antagonists see the female they immediately trot towards her; but, coming in sight of each other, there is usually a pause, during which the shaking of the tail, the flapping of the ears, and the lifting of the trunk manifest a state of extreme disquiet. The object of contention does not attempt to quit her post, but stands, with evident tokens of pleasure, mutely contemplating the approaching struggle. After a short interval one of the elephants rushes to the encounter; and when both meet, the shock is always tremendous. The tusks come into stunning collision, and with so loud a shock as to be heard at a distance of several hundred yards, the concussion being so tremendous as to raise the two gigantic champions off their fore-legs. After they have met, the contest sometimes becomes terrible in the extreme. They grasp one another's trunks, butting with their heads, and occasionally raising a shrill cry of the fiercest rage. The female, meanwhile, does not offer to interpose, but calmly surveys the combat, as if with the gratifying consciousness that her presence stimulates the gallant rivals to maintain the desperate struggle for victory.

After a while the weaker elephant invariably gives way; for, the moment these creatures become sensible of their inferiority, they seem at once to be aware that the chances of success are against them, and immediately relinquish the encounter. When this is the case he usually turns, and makes a sudden retreat, pursued by the victor, which sometimes applies his tusks so forcibly to the rear of his retreating adversary as to leave indelible marks of his strength, and frequently to shake the mahoot from the network, to which he had clung during the contest.

When the elephants are equally matched, they continue

striking at each other's heads, bringing their tusks into such violent contact as often snaps them close to the jaw; thus, in a manner, disabling the sufferer for the rest of his life, as the jaw generally becomes diseased after so severe a fracture, and in many cases to such an extent that it is found necessary to destroy the animal.

When the contest appears likely to terminate fatally, rockets are thrown between the competitors. Of these they have a great dread; nevertheless, in some instances, so implacable is their fury that the rockets fail to separate them; in which case they are attacked in the rear with long spears by men on horseback, who strike them so sharply that they turn upon their assailants, whom they pursue with all the rage of baffled determination, often putting the horses of their tormentors to their utmost speed ere the latter can escape the threatened vengeance of their maddened pursuers. The female is now withdrawn, and the object of excitement being no longer in view, the mahoots have little difficulty in persuading their charges to retire peaceably from the scene of contention.

I remember once seeing, at an entertainment of this kind, three wild buffaloes driven into the arena against an elephant. In order to render them the more fierce, crackers were fastened to their tails. During the explosion of these, the terrified animals ran to and fro as if in a state of frenzy, and one of them charged the elephant, which stood in a corner of the square, with the blind and misguided fury of madness. The colossal creature watched his victim as it plunged desperately forward, calmly awaiting its approach with his head depressed, and the point of his tusks brought to a level with the shoulders of his advancing foe. The buffalo rushed onward, and was almost instantly impaled; the elephant casting the writhing body from his tusks, and then coolly crushing it with his fore-feet.

The two other buffaloes, having now somewhat recovered from the terror excited by the crackers, which had hitherto diverted their attention from the elephant, gazed wildly round the enclosure, and, seeing their enemy prepared for a charge, pawed the ground, raising the dust, and flinging the earth over their heads with their hoofs in a continued shower; then erecting their tails, with a loud roar they simultaneously charged the elephant, which still remained in the corner where he had at first stationed himself. He eyed them with a deliberate but keen glance, placing his head, as before, towards the ground, and bringing those terrible instruments of destruction with which his jaws were armed in a position to meet the charge of his foremost foe. The result was precisely the same as in the former attack, the buffalo being instantly transfixed upon the elephant's tusks; but before the victor could release them from their incumbrance, the second buffalo was upon him. With the quickness of thought, however, he raised his fore-leg and struck his assailant between the horns, rolling it over and instantly crushing it to death.

It sometimes, indeed, happens in these encounters when the elephant is timid, which is the natural character of this animal, that he is dreadfully gored by his furious assailants, to which he offers no resistance, but flies from them in great terror. An old elephant is generally too wary and too conscious of his own strength to allow himself to be subdued by such inferior adversaries, and when he offers a resolute resistance, the buffaloes invariably fare the worst. But at these cruel exhibitions, however the contest terminates, there is much more distress than enjoyment experienced—at least, by European spectators, to whom the sight of a violent death inflicted even upon animals which they naturally hold in dread is, in most cases, a spectacle altogether shocking to the better feelings of humanity. On the occasion to which I have just referred, after the contest between the elephant and buffaloes, a bear was introduced

L

before the party assembled to witness the sports, and a man undertook to encounter it without any arms, save a gauntlet made of buffalo horn, called a jetty.

The bear was a large one of its species, and had been kept without food for two days, in order to render it the more fierce. When first released from its den, it paced the ground with a sullen aspect, occasionally looking up at the spectators and uttering a low dismal roar, but showed no symptoms of positive exasperation. The moment the man entered, it paused, erected itself on its hind legs, and yelled loudly. The Hindoo was a tall, powerful young man, with extremely long arms, a fine expansive chest, and a clear beaming eye, expressive of cool determination and wary caution. He first commenced operations by walking round his adversary, sometimes advancing, then retreating—now quickening his pace, then suddenly stopping, all the while distracting the attention of his angry foe by numerous contortions of body, occasionally clapping his hands, striking his chest, and springing from the ground with an agility which would have surprised the most accomplished 'maître de ballet' in Europe.

His shaggy opponent, at length becoming enraged, advanced upon him with a shriek of rage, and extended a paw to grasp his hip: but the Hindoo, with the rapidity of lightning, planted a blow upon the bear's cheek, which cut open the skin, and sent Bruin staggering several paces backwards. The poor animal seemed for a moment stunned with surprise, and before it could recover it received another tremendous hit on the muzzle, which caused it to turn and run to the corner of the enclosure. After shaking its nose and sneezing, it once more erected its body, having now its back supported by the bamboo railings. The man tried by all sorts of gesticulations, suddenly retreating and falling down, to draw his adversary from its position, but in vain. The animal was evidently aware of the advantage of presenting to its antagonist only one point of attack, and therefore would not budge from its corner; but, covering its head with its large shaggy paws, the Hindoo champion found it extremely difficult to deliver a blow where it would be likely to be effectual. Finding that he could not rouse the bear, he sprang forward and gave it a smart kick in the flank: this caused the animal suddenly to depress its paws; in an instant, the jetty was rattling on its head with a severity which caused it to yell for several seconds. It now lay on the earth with its muzzle in the corner, and its back towards its conqueror, who, disdaining to strike a fallen enemy, made his salaam to the spectators with a grace peculiar to all the Eastern races, and retired from the scene of combat amidst their unanimous acclamations. The bear was a good deal punished, but its skull was too hard to be cracked with the blow of a fist.

The defeat of the bear was followed by an exhibition of a different order. A slight but firm ladder, composed of bamboo, was placed upright on the ground within the area, a strong pole crossing the top at right angles; from the end of this pole two stout cords depended, which were tightened to stay the ladder, the ends being staked into the ground in such a manner that the apparatus could not give way. A small muscular Hindoo was then introduced, naked to the waist, dressed only in a pair of short white trousers, which extended half-way down his thighs. The muscles of his arms were of prodigious size, while those of his legs were small in the comparison. He wore no turban, but a gay skull-cap composed of yellow and pale blue silk. From each ear depended a large plain gold ring.

Upon entering, the little man made his salaam to the audience; then, rubbing his palms together for a few moments, he bounded towards the ladder, and, grasping the first bar above his head with both hands, mounted with astonishing activity, keeping his feet all the while perfectly motionless, and at least six inches from the frame. Having raised himself by his hands alone to the transverse pole, by a sudden jerk of his body he threw his feet upward, and was in a moment seen resting upon his head with his arms crossed over his bosom and his legs closed, forming an inverted triangle from the shoulders to the toes. He continued in this position for upwards of a minute without the slightest motion, appearing as if he had been suddenly converted into stone, amid the shouts of an applauding multitude. When he had sufficiently rested himself after the toil of climbing, a strong cord was flung to him from below, which he caught, and drew from the ground a ball, apparently about six pounds weight, of solid iron : it was enclosed in a stout netting of twine, to which the cord was securely attached.

Having drawn up the ball to within about three yards from his hand, the dexterous Hindoo, who remained still upon his head, gradually swung it backward and forward until he was able to describe the entire circle, when, swinging it round three several times, he elanced it from his grasp, sending it over the heads of the spectators to the distance of seventy-five paces—at least sixty yards. He now lowered his legs, and placed himself upon his back along the pole. When he had perfectly secured his equilibrium, six creases or daggers, with broad double-edged blades, were thrown to him ; these he caught successively with great dexterity, still maintaining his horizontal position upon the transverse bamboo. When he had possessed himself of the six daggers, he threw them one after the other several yards above his head, catching them as they fell, four always being in the air at the same instant ; and this he continued for the space of at least two minutes, at length letting them drop one by one on his body, the handle invariably coming in contact with it, and the blade being always uppermost.

The performer next took an iron rod about three feet long, and, standing erect upon the pole, placed the rod in the centre, and upon the top of it a shallow wooden bowl. With a sudden spring he seated himself in the bowl, balancing the rod so accurately that it did not appear to move a hair's breadth out of the perpendicular. In this situation twelve brass balls were flung to him; these he caught and projected into the air, keeping them in perpetual motion for several minutes: he then sprang upon his feet, standing in the bowl, without allowing a single ball to reach the ground. When this had been continued for another interval of two or three minutes, he leaped upon the bamboo, the iron rod and its wooden crown falling at the same instant to the ground. The little man concluded this clever exhibition by descending the ladder upon his hands head foremost amid the shouts of the assembled multitude.

After several other displays of skill, the sports concluded by a native throwing a quoit at a mark with astonishing force and precision. The quoit used on this occasion was somewhat flatter than that generally employed in the rustic games of Europe: it was more delicately shaped, and had a sharp cutting edge all round the exterior circle. The quoit-thrower was a short but stout man, nearly as black as an African, his whole body covered with hair, and his countenance extremely stern and forbidding.

A wooden frame being placed at one end of the enclosure, with three white lines marked upon it, an inch and a half broad, the quoit-thrower stood at least twenty yards from the mark, and, having fixed the quoit upon the forefinger of his right hand, he whirled it round for several seconds, and then discharged it with amazing velocity at the wooden frame, striking the centre line, and impelling it above an inch into the wood, in which the disk stuck so firmly as to require a considerable tug to withdraw it. This he repeated twice, striking the second and third white lines with equal dexterity and force.

A pine-apple was next suspended from a pole at the same distance, at which the man discharged his missile, cutting the fruit completely through the centre; thus showing that this simple instrument may be used with great effect in native warfare, in which it is occasionally employed.

The natives of Hindostan are celebrated throughout the East for their feats of manual skill; in these I think they are unequalled by the inhabitants of any other country. Their strength, too, in some instances is perfectly amazing, when we consider the homely diet upon which they feed, and the attenuating climate in which they dwell.

The Storm

THE STORM

By Adelaide Anne Procter

The Tempest rages wild and high,
The waves lift up their voice and cry
Fierce answers to the angry sky ;
                Miserere Domine.

Through the black night and driving rain,
A ship is struggling, all in vain,
To live upon the stormy main ;
                Miserere Domine.

The thunders roar, the lightnings glare,
Vain is it now to strive or dare ;
A cry goes up of great despair ;
                Miserere Domine.

The stormy voices of the main,
The roaring wind, the pelting rain
Beat on the nursery window-pane ;
                Miserere Domine.

Warm-curtained was the little bed,
Soft pillowed was the little head ;
'The storm will wake the child,' they said ;
                Miserere Domine.

Cowering among his pillows white,
He prays, his blue eyes dim with fright,
'Father! save those at sea to-night;'
    Miserere Domine.

The morning shone all clear and gay
On a ship at anchor in the bay,
And on a little child at play;
    Gloria tibi Domine!

AN INTERESTING EVENT

By W. M. Thackeray

SITTING the other day alone at dinner at the club, and at the next table to Smith, who was in conversation with his friend Jones, I could not but overhear their colloquy, or, rather, Mr. Smith's communication to his friend. As, after all, it betrays no secrets of private life; as his adventure, such as it is, may happen to any one of us; and as, above all, the story is not in the least moral or instructive, I took the liberty of writing it down, as follows:—

'I could not go to that dinner at the Topham Sawyers,' Smith remarked, 'where you met the Duke, and where Beaumoris sat next to Miss Henrica Hays (whom I certainly should have manœuvred to hand down to dinner, and of course should have had as good a chance as Bo of proposing for her, of being accepted, and getting a wife notoriously consumptive, and with six thousand a-year),—I could not go to the Topham Sawyers, because I had accepted an invitation to dine with my old schoolfellow Budgeon. He lives near Hyde Park Gardens, in the Tyburn quarter. He does not give dinners often, and I make it a point, when I have promised to go to a man—dammy, sir, I make it a point not to throw him over.'

Jones here remarked that the wine was with Smith, which the other acknowledged by filling up a bumper, and then resumed:—

'I knew that the Budgeons had asked a large party, and, indeed, all their crack people ; for I had seen Mrs. Budgeon in the Park the day before, driving by the Serpentine in her open carriage, and looking uncommonly interesting. She had her best folks,—she mentioned them ; nor did I forget to let her know that I was myself invited to the Topham Sawyers on the same day,—for there is no use in making yourself too cheap ; and if you *do* move about in a decent circle, Jones, my boy, I advise you to let your friends know it.'

Jones observed that he thought the claret was corked, and the filberts were fine. Smith continued:—

'I do not always array myself in a white neckcloth and waistcoat to go to dinner, Jones, but I think it is right on grand days to do so—I think it's right. Well, sir, I put myself into my very best fig, embroidered shirt, white waistcoat, turquoise buttons, white stockings, and that sort of thing, and set out for Budgeon's at a quarter to eight. I dressed here at the Club. My fool of a servant had not brought me any white gloves though ; so I was obliged to buy a pair for three-and-sixpence, as we drove by Houbigant's.

'I recollect that it was the thirty-first of June, and, as a matter of course, it was pouring with rain. By the way, do you *bake* your white neckcloths in damp weather, Jones ? It's the only way to keep 'em right.'

Jones said he thought this was a better bottle than the last.

'I drove up, sir, to Budgeon's door at Hyde Park Gardens, and of course had a row with the scoundrelly cabman about his fare. I gave him eighteenpence ; he said a gentleman would have given him half-a-crown. "Confound your impudence, sir !" said I. "Vell," said the impudent brute, "vell, I never said you vos one." At this moment Budgeon's door was opened by Cobb, his butler. Cobb was still in pepper-and-salt trousers, which surprised me. He looked rather dubiously at me in the cab.

'"Am I late?" says I.

'"No, sir; only—you haven't got your note? But my master will see *you*, sir. You stop here, cab."

'And quitting the vehicle, of which the discontented rascal of a driver still persisted in saying, that "a gentleman would gimmy 'alf-a-crownd," I entered Mr. Budgeon's house, splashing my white stockings in the mud as I went in, to the accompaniment of a hee-haw from the brute on the cab box. The familiarity of the people, sir, is disgusting.

'I was troubled as I entered. The two *battants* of the hall-door were not cast open; the fellows in black were not there to bawl out your name up the stairs; there was only Cobb, in a dirty Marsella waistcoat, jingling his watch-chain.

'"Good Heavens, Cobb!" says I—for I was devilish hungry—"what has happened?" And I began to think (for I have heard Budgeon is rather shaky) that there was an execution in the house.

'"Missis, sir—little girl, sir—about three o'clock, sir—master will see you—Mr. Smith, sir." And with these words Cobb ushered me into the dining-room, where Budgeon sat alone.

'There was not the least preparation for a grand dinner, as you may suppose. It is true that a soiled and crumpled bit of old table-cloth was spread at one corner of the table, with one knife and fork laid; but the main portion of the mahogany was only covered with its usual green baize, and Budgeon sat at a farther end in his dressing gown, and writing letter after letter. They are a very numerous family. She was a Miss Walkinghame,—one of the Wiltshire Walkinghames. You know her name is Fanny Decima, and I don't know how far the teens in the family went. Budgeon has five sisters himself, and he was firing off notes to all these amiable relatives when I came in.

They were all, as you may suppose, pretty much to the same effect :—

' "My dear Maria" (or Eliza, or Louisa, according to circumstances), "I write a hasty line to say that our dear Fanny has just made me a present of a fifth little girl. Dr. Bloxam is with her, and I have the happiness to say that they are both doing perfectly well. With best regards to Hickson" (or Thompson, or Jackson, as the case and the brother-in-law may be), "I am, my dear, &c., affectionately yours, Leonard Budgeon."

'Twenty-three of these letters to relatives, besides thirty-eight to put off the dinner and evening party, Budgeon had written; and he bragged about it as if he had done a great feat. For my part, I thought, with rage, that the Topham Sawyers' dinner was coming off at that minute and that I might have been present but for this disagreeable *contretemps*.

' "You're come in time to wish me joy!" says Budgeon, looking up from his *paperasses* in a piteous tone and manner.

' "Joy, indeed!" says I. In fact I wished him at Bath.

' "I'm so accustomed to this sort of thing," said he, "that I'm no longer excited by it at all. You'll stay and dine with me, now you're come."

'I looked daggers at him! I might have dined at the Topham Sawyers, I said, but for this sudden arrival.

' "What is there for dinner, Cobb? You'll lay a cover for Mr. Smith."

'Cobb looked grave. "The cook is gone to fetch Mrs. Walkinghame. I've kep the cab to go to Queen Charlotte's Hospital for—for the nuss. Buttons is gone out with the notes, sir. The young ladies' maid has taken them to their haunt Codger's; the other female servants is busy upstairs with missis, sir."

' "Do you mean there's no dinner?" cries Budgeon, looking as if he was relieved though. "Well, I have written the notes. Bloxam says my wife is on no account to be disturbed; and I tell you what, Smith, you shall give me a dinner at the Club."

'"Very good," I growled out; although it is deuced hard to be obliged to give a dinner when you have actually refused the Topham Sawyers. And Cobb, going to his master's dressing-room, returned thence with the coat, hat, and umbrella, with which that gentleman usually walks abroad.

'"Come along," said I, with the best grace; and we were both going out accordingly, when suddenly the door opened, and Mrs. Wake, Mrs. Budgeon's maid, who has been with her ever since she was born, made her appearance.

'A man who has in his house a lady's maid who has been with his wife ever since she was born, has probably two tyrants, certainly one, over him. I would not take a girl with ten thousand a-year and a maid who has been with her from the nursery. If your wife is not jealous of you, that woman is. If your wife does not know when you slip in from the Club, after midnight, that woman is awake, depend upon it, and hears you go upstairs. If, under pretence of a long debate in the House of Commons, you happen to go to Greenwich with a bachelor party, that woman finds the Trafalgar bill in your pocket, and somehow hears of your *escapade*. You fancy yourself very independent and unobserved, and that you carry on, you rogue! quite snugly and quietly through life. Fool! you are environed by spies, and circumvented by occult tyrants. Your friends' servants and your own know all that you do. Your wife's maid has intelligences with all the confidential females and males of your circle. You are pursued by detectives in plain (some in second-hand) clothes, and your secrets are as open to them as the area-gate by which they enter your house. Budgeon's eye quailed before that severe light blue one which hawk-beaked Mrs. Wake fixed upon him.

'"You are not a going out, sir?" said that woman, in a cracked voice.

'"Why, Wake, I was going to—to dine at the Club with Mr. Smith; that's all,—with Mr. Smith, you know!" and so, of course, *I* was dragged in.

'"I'll tell my missis, sir, that Mr. Smith wished to take you away; though I'm sure he didn't know her situation, and a blessed baby born only five hours, and the medical man in the house."

'"Hang it!" says I, "I never asked—I—that is——"

'"O! I dessay, sir, it was master as ast hisself," Mrs. Wake answered. "And my poor missis upstairs, and I've been with her ever since she was born, and took her from the month,—that I did, and *I* won't desert her now. But I won't answer for her life, nor Dr. Bloxam won't, if master should go out now, as you are a goin' to, sir."

'"Good Heavens, Wake! why shouldn't I? There's no dinner for me. You turned me out of Mrs. Budgeon's room when I went upstairs, and ordered me not to come up again."

'"She's not to be disturbed on no account, sir. The dear suffering think," Mrs. Wake said. "Her *mar* is coming and will soon be year, that's *one* comfort, and will keep you company."

'"Oh yes, Mrs. Walkinghame," Budgeon ruefully said. "Where is she to sleep, Wake?"

'"In the best bedroom, sir; in course, in the yellow room, sir," Wake answered.

'"And—and where am I to go?" asked the gentleman.

'"Your things is halready brought down into the study, and you're to sleep on the sofy and harm-chair, of course, sir," the other said.

'Budgeon, now, is a very stout, bulky little man, the

"sofy" is only a rout-seat, and the arm-chair is what you call a Glastonbury—an oak chair ornamented with middle-age gim-cracks, and about as easy as Edward the Confessor's fauteuil in Westminster Abbey. I pictured the wretch to myself, stretched out on a couch which a fakeer or a hermit would find hard to lie on.

'"Oh, thank you!" was all the cowed slave could say; and I saw at once, from his behaviour to that supercilious female, and the bewildered obedience which he appeared to bestow on her, that there was some secret between them which rendered the domestic the mistress of her employer I wonder what it could have been, Jones? She had read private letters out of his waistcoat pocket, very likely. At any rate, my dear fellow, when you marry, take care to have no secrets, or of submitting to an inquisitor over you in the shape of a lady's maid.'

Jones (who, by the way, is not, I should say, a man of much conversational power) just thanked Smith to pass the bottle; and the latter resumed his harrowing narrative.

'As we were conversing in the above manner, there came a banging knock at the door,—one of those coarse, vulgar, furious peals which a cabman, imitating a footman, endeavours to perform. We all started guiltily as we heard it. It was most likely some outlying guest who, like myself, had not received his note of excuse, and had come forth to partake of Budgeon's most Barmecidal entertainment.

'"And you haven't even a-tied up the knocker!" said Mrs. Wake, with a look of withering scorn. The knocker had slipped his memory, Budgeon owned. At which the maid said "Of course." Of course she said of course.

'Now Mrs. Wake, looking savagely round her and round the room, saw on the table my Gibus' hat, which I had set down there, and in it my bran-new white gloves, that I had bought at Houbigant's for three-and-sixpence. A savage satisfaction lighted up her eyes as she viewed them, and diving down into her pocket, and producing thence a piece of string, this fiend in human shape seized hold of my gloves with a sarcastic apology, and said she was sure I would have no objection to her tying up the knocker with them, and preventing her missis from being knocked to death. So she sailed out of the room with my three-and-sixpence in her hands, and, being a tall, bony woman, who could reach up to the knockers without difficulty, she had each of them soon muffled up in a beautiful white French kid, No. 8½.

'"You see how it is, old boy," Budgeon dismally said. "Fanny doesn't like my leaving the house; and, in her delicate condition, of course, we must humour her. I must come and dine with you some other day. We have plenty of time before us, you know. And to-night I must stop and receive my mother-in-law and take a mutton-chop at home."

'"Take a mutton-chop at home indeed!" The wretched man little knew what truth he was telling there; for I give you my honour, sir, five minutes afterwards, Mrs. Wake, having finished tying up the door with my gloves, and all the other servants of the house being absent upon various errands connected with the interesting occasion, she reappeared amongst us, holding an uncovered dish, on which there were two cold mutton-chops left from the children's dinner! And I left the unhappy man to eat these, and went away to devour my own chagrin.

'It was pouring with rain, sir, as I went down the street. There are no cabs within a mile of Hyde Park Gardens; and I was soon wet through, and my shirt-front and cravat all rumpled with rain; otherwise I might have gone into a tavern and dined, and slipped into the Topham Sawyers in the evening. But I was too great a figure for that; and I was forced, positively, to come back to this Club to take my morning clothes out of the bag, and reassume them, and to dine here at my own charge, after having refused one of the best dinners in London.'

'Is that all, old boy?' Jones asked.

'All! no, it isn't all!' said Smith, with a horrid shriek of laughter. 'Look here, sir.' And he pulled out a note, which he read, and which was to the following effect :—

'" Dear Smith,—You were the first person in the house after an interesting event occurred there, and Fanny and I have agreed that you must be godfather to our little stranger. Both are doing very well, and your little god-daughter elect is pronounced by the authorities to be the prettiest and largest child ever seen of her age.

'"Mrs. Walkinghame is still with us, and Wake allows me to go out sometimes. When will you give me the dinner you promised me at the Megatherium? We might go to Vauxhall afterwards, where Van Amburgh, I am told, is very interesting and worth seeing.

'" Yours ever, dear Smith,
'" LEONARD BUDGEON."

'There, sir,' cried Smith, 'isn't that enough to try any man's patience? Just tot up what that "interesting event" has cost me—not the dinner to Budgeon, who is a good fellow, and I don't grudge it to him—but the rest. Cabs, four shillings; gloves, three-and-six; Henrica Hays, whom I might have had with two hundred thousand pounds; and add to this a silver mug or a papboat, which will cost me four or five pound, and a couple of guineas to that vixen of a Mrs. Wake;—and all coming from an interesting event.'

'Suppose we have coffee?' Jones remarked. And as I could not listen decently any more to their conversation, I laid down the newspaper and walked away.

A SUMMER DAY

By J. Dodds

SUNRISE—FORENOON

The sun is rising, and an eastern breeze
Is blowing freshness through the waving trees;
The air is kindling into rosy light,
And Day rides forth in flaming chariot bright.

Thick-sown with freshening dew the meadow lies,
And misty vapours from the valley rise,
To curl like robes around the mountains dun,
Then melt away before the thirsty sun.

The rural revelry, that rang the while
The husbandman began his pleasant toil,
Now dies away, and Industry severe
In peace pursues the labours of the year.

The herds have settled to their pastures green,
An animated, yet a quiet scene;
Along the flowery sward they slowly pass,
And revel on the richness of the grass.

So silent grows the day, that even the bird
Among the rustling leaves is clearly heard,
And the sweet murmur of the tiny stream
That wild flowers shelter from the solar beam.

Windsor Park

Now the clear sun looks fiercely down, and soon
Will he be mounted on the tower of noon;
The massy shadow of yon stately tree
Glooms like a dark isle in a tropic sea.

NOON

Now comes the calm luxurious hour of rest,
By all the panting sons of labour blest;
Sweet at this burning season, doubly sweet
To all who mingle in its toil and heat.

The humming beech-tree shadow o'er him cast,
The sun-burnt hedger sits at his repast,
Like monarch at a feast; with relish rare
He banquets on his poor, unseasoned fare.

The lambs that sported, and the ewes that fed,
The morning long, now seek the rustic shed,
Or by the shady margin of the wood,
They rest, and o'er their past regalement brood.

In fine, all creatures of the earth and air,
Oppressed and panting, to the shade repair,
And feel it all their luxury to shun
The torrid splendour of the lofty sun.

Beside the secret and dark-shaded bank,
With dewy flowers and undried verdure rank,
The pensive stripling seeks the waters cool,
And plunges, swan-like, in the quiet pool.

The aged shepherd, on the mountain side
Stretched thoughtfully, beholds a prospect wide;
A stunted thorn its shadow o'er him flings,
And at his feet a bubbling fountain springs.

There doth the rustic sage untroubled lie,
And ponder much untaught philosophy;
With look of silent rapture he surveys
The pictured valley lying in a blaze.

By Nature's best inheritance 'tis his;
Thence he derives a heritage of bliss.
Though but the master of an humble fold,
His the delight, another's is the gold.

AFTERNOON—NIGHT

But now the woodman, lively after rest,
Resumes his toil upon the mountain's breast,
And with a blithesome, oft-repeated tune,
Beguiles the long and sunny afternoon.

By the wild brook, among its rushy bowers,
The little village maidens gather flowers.
To their charmed sense, the beauteous buds they hold
Are dearer far than fairy gems of gold.

Without a tear—yet grief too soon will come—
They sport, nor is their merry pastime dumb;
So lovely in their fleeting lives, they seem
Like water-lilies floating down a stream.

These sportive children of the laughing eye,
And brow serene as the unclouded sky,
Run gracefully, and shout, and look behind,
Their bright locks playing in the summer wind.

But tired with shouting sport, and mirth's excess,
They fling themselves, in careless loveliness,
Upon the green sward, and with half-shut eyes
They sing old rhymes and rural melodies.

So may we deem, in heaven's serener clime,
That tender children, snatched away from time,
Enjoy eternity in blooming bowers,
And sing God's glory amid streams and flowers.

But lo ! a darkening cloud of softest rain
Falls, like a pearly veil, upon the plain.
The glittering fields rejoice in greenest hue,
And all the air is moistened with a dew.

With lovely strength looks forth the setting sun,
As one whose glorious race is nearly run ;
The clouds around him, by his splendour riven,
Glow like the golden battlements of heaven.

A universal song is in the woods,
A pleasant voice comes from the sylvan floods ;
The evening breeze is odorous and bland,
And starry Night beholds a quiet land.

Source of our life, and Giver of our days !
Let me, at morn and eve, thy glory praise ;
And when these earthly years have passed away,
May I enjoy an endless Summer day.

ROUEN

From Saint Catherine's Hill

In his Notes on his Turner Drawings, exhibited at the Gallery of the Fine Arts Society in 1878, Mr. Ruskin says: 'Of the Seine subjects, fortune gave me the " Rouen," the mightiest piece of work in my collection next to the " Golden Bough." It is beyond all wonder for easy minuteness and harmony of power, perfectly true and like the place ; also inestimable as a type of Turner's consummate work. If any foreign master of landscape-painting, hitherto unacquainted with Turner, wishes to know his essential strength, let him study this simple drawing and try to do something like it.'

The windings of the Seine, with its wooded island and its many-arched bridges, and with the little sailing boats dotted on its surface ; the pleasing foreground with its hay-waggon, and the troops of visitors climbing the hill ; the towers of the distant cathedral, and of St. Ouen standing amidst the clustered houses ; the level country on the right bank of the river, the distant hills ; and, above all, the lovely sky, one of the most beautiful Turner ever painted, make up a picture which the veriest tyro in art must admire, and we cannot wonder at the value that is put upon it by its present possessor, as a work of superlative workmanship.

The engraving by William Miller, of Edinburgh, is one of the very best of all the reproductions in black and white of Turner's drawings. It first appeared in the second volume of 'Turner's Annual Tour' in the year 1834, and afterwards was reprinted in 'The Rivers of France.' The impression before us shows how well a steel-plate, when properly engraved, will last; there is but little difference in the prints after many years of wear.

WILLIAM COLLINS, R.A.

By Richard Redgrave, R.A.

WHILE it is given to but few, very few, artists to attain the highest rank in art, it is an honourable end to have stamped a marked individuality on any of its varied modes of appealing to mankind. If the former was denied to William Collins, R.A., it at least was given to him to find a somewhat untrodden path in art for himself, and to make the latter success his own by the way he treated his subjects. William Collins was born in Great Titchfield Street, on the 18th September, 1788. Although an Englishman by birth, by parentage he was allied to each of the sister kingdoms; his mother being a native of Edinburgh, and his father born at Wicklow in Ireland. The elder Collins had settled in England as a writer and journalist, and to these, considering them as precarious means of supporting his family, he added the business of a picture-dealer. The love of landscape scenery in the younger Collins might be derived from both parents, born as they were in places remarkable for picturesque beauty. The two sons, William and Francis, moreover, were from their father's business early thrown among art and artists; and brought up in its very atmosphere, what wonder that William, the elder, chose it for his pursuit in life? His first studies, we are told, were from the objects around him, and these alternated with 'copies of pictures and drawings for the small patrons and dealers of the day.'

Collins' father was intimate, among others, with George Morland (an intimacy which subsequently led to his writing the life of that artist); and the son was very anxious to be introduced to a man who was everywhere spoken of as a wonder of erratic genius, and who had promised to admit the lad to his studio, that he might at least see the conduct of his pictures. It so happened that the boy's first sight of the famous animal painter was at his father's house, under very questionable circumstances, sleeping off, in the kitchen, a fit of filthy intoxication; this may have been a lesson for our young painter, who was through life a man of most correct habits. From this time Collins was a visitor at Morland's painting-room as often as the irregularities of that painter would permit. He seems to have had a high sense of his talents, and to have taken great interest in the places where he had been in company with Morland when in after-life he revisited them. We are told, however, that he did not consider that he gained any remarkable advantage in the practical part of his art from the kind of instruction which Morland was able to convey; but those who examine the works of the two men will see that the early impression made by the art of the eccentric painter had a marked influence on the future art of Collins, and perhaps first led him to those rustic subjects which he handled so skilfully, and treated with a refinement which was denied to the man of gross sensuality and intemperate habits.

Pursuing his desultory studies under his father's superintendence, alternately painting from a group of objects, perchance jars or blacking-bottles, with his friend John Linnell; sketching from nature and copying pictures spurious and original, with the advantage also of seeing the rapid pencil of Morland at work to produce means to continue his excesses, young Collins reached his nineteenth year, and was sufficiently advanced in 1807 to obtain admission as a student in the Royal Academy, and also fortuitously to become an exhibitor on its walls. Of these first pictures, 'Two Views of Millbank,' there is no record further than their insertion in the catalogue.

In 1809 Collins was advanced to the life-school, and in the same year his pictures, both in the Academy and in the British Institution, obtained some share of public notice ; and, what was even of more importance to a struggling artist fighting his own way in life, they found purchasers also. As years passed on, young Collins improved in his art, though not rapidly ; his works had little of the richness and less of the free handling he arrived at afterwards. Early in the year 1812 Collins lost a father to whom he seems to have been tenderly attached ; a short diary of this period, preserved by his son, very touchingly paints the few anxious days which preceded his death, and the destitution of the family now left wholly dependent on the young painter. But friends rose up to help, as they mostly do for those who are true-hearted, and we find one kind friend coming forward to assist them with furniture in lieu of that which the creditors had laid their hands on ; while another, Sir Thomas Heathcote, one of Collins' first patrons, not only paid him half the price of a picture in advance, but offered a loan of money in addition. From this time, in young Collins' pictures, the figures were more predominant than the landscape ; his subjects, mostly the joys and sorrows of children, won their way in public estimation, and seem to have found ready purchasers.

It shows how popular were the subjects of his choice, and how true it is that the quality of colour in art is the most attractive to the public ; and when joined to subjects appealing, as did those of Collins, to the heart and understanding of all, is sure to win an early success. Both these qualities were united in a work of this period which became very widely popular, and is a representative work of the

Woodbury-Gravure.

painter's, 'The Sale of the Pet Lamb,' which, painted in 1812, united very happily the best characteristics of the painter's art.

The incident is one of frequent occurrence in rural life, where the *cade* lamb, as it is called—a lamb which by accident has lost its dam—is given away to the cottager, that it may be petted into life, if possible, by the active sympathy of his children : it gradually grows into their young hearts as companion and playmate, until its age, or some pressing need, gives it up to the usual fate of its kind. In the painter's treatment of the subject, the butcher-lad has come to lead away the unconscious victim ; he does his duty kindly for the children's sake, although (as labouring in his vocation) *he* is untouched by any sentiment the others feel. One of the children pushes him away from their playfellow, another feeds it for the last time, while a girl clings to the mother, who is receiving the price of the lamb, tearfully urging that it should not be taken from them. This picture, with one or two others of the same class, so advanced Collins in the estimation of his brother-artists that in November, 1814, he was elected an associate of the Royal Academy.

The painter, having obtained his first promotion in art, had taken a new and larger house ; but although his works were popular and many were purchased, he had still difficulties to struggle with ; in subsequent years fortune was not equally favourable, and we find an entry in his diary in the spring of 1816 :—' A black-looking April day, with one sixpence in my pocket, 700*l*. in debt, shabby clothes, a fine house, and a large stock of my own handiworks.' It must be remembered that the young painter had his mother and his brother at this time to provide for, that he had entered upon the responsibilities of a larger establishment, and also that, on looking down the list of pictures and their prices, recorded in his *Life*, it is evident from statements in his diaries, that some of the pictures were not purchased at the time they were painted, but afterwards, when he was growing still more into fame and notice.

In the troubles of this period of his life, he cast about for some new class of subjects to attract the attention of the public, and made journeys to the sea-coast, painting first at Cromer, and afterwards at Hastings, coast scenery, enlivened with groups of fisher-boys, boats, fish, &c.; these he treated with great freshness and truth, and having made himself a place of his own in art, he was elected a full member of the academic body in February, 1820. In 1822, during a visit to Scotland in company with his friend Wilkie, Collins completed a long-standing engagement by marrying Miss Geddes, by whom he had two sons. The elder has written a life of his father, full of matters of interest both to artists and to the general public.

Collins was now well established, having obtained the highest honours of the profession, and having in his particular branch of landscape art, as Wilkie told him, the ball at his feet, he had but to paint as he had begun to widen his popularity. There was no fear of any lack of subjects in the inexhaustible field he had chosen, nor of their palling on the public taste. Such subjects he continued to paint until the year 1836, when he produced two of his very best works—'Sunday Morning,' and 'Happy as a King.' This latter picture is full of life and action, the landscape is broad and simple in manner, and is beautifully suggestive.

Wilkie, while on the Continent, had in his letters repeatedly urged his friend to see the beauties of Italy: recounting the many subjects he would find there for his pencil, and the desirableness of filling his mind with new ideas; and at length Collins made up his mind to the journey, and on the 19th September, 1836, he left England to spend some time in the South.

To us who look back over his whole course and review his art life, it may be permitted to doubt if the Italian journey was at all beneficial to his reputation. It is true that some beautiful landscapes resulted from it; such as that seen 'From the Caves of Ulysses at Sorrento, Bay of Naples,' a work of great truth and beauty. But Collins was essentially an English painter; from his youth up he had lived among the rustic children he loved to paint and the rural scenery in which he placed them; and although Italian mendicants, priests, and lazzaroni might be a change to the public, yet even at the time they were hardly thought a change for the better; while to ourselves, such pictures as 'Happy as a King' and 'Rustic Civility' are worth all the figure-pictures, the fruits of his Italian journey. Nor can we forget that to the treacherous smiles of an Italian sun we ultimately owed the loss of the artist. While at Sorrento he could not be persuaded that it was dangerous to paint out of doors in the heat of the day. The temptation to do so was great; the artist was incapable of idleness, and continued against the remonstrances of his friends to work at all hours; the result was a severe attack of rheumatic fever, which lasted many weeks, and left behind it a disease of the heart, which troubled him during the remaining years of his life, and finally resulted in his death on the 17th February, 1847.

LETITIA ELIZABETH LANDON

By William Howitt

(*Written in* 1839)

We have, within a few years, felt some of the most vivid sensations which the death of popular writers can, under any circumstances, possibly create. We have not forgotten the electric shock which the death of Byron, falling in his prime and in a noble cause, sent through Europe: nor the more expected, but not less solemn and strongly recognised departure of Sir Walter Scott: but neither of these exceeded that with which the news was received of the sudden decease of the still young and popular poetess, L. E. L. The apprehensions which the climate suggested, on the first tidings of her going out to Cape Coast Castle, did not even abate the abrupt effect of the news of her death. The mysterious circumstances attending it threw a tragic horror around it, and kindled an intense eagerness to penetrate their obscurity. The strange contrast between the youthful and buoyant spirit of L. E. L.'s genius, and the sombre tone of her views of life and human nature, were not more startling and stimulant than that between her popularity and her fate.

It is not our intention here to pause over this sudden quenching of so lovely and brilliant a luminary, nor to attempt to dissipate a single mystery which hangs over it. The subject of L. E. L.'s first volume was love—a subject

LETITIA ELIZABETH LANDON (L.E.L.)

By Daniel Maclise, R.A.

which we might have supposed, in one so young, would have been clothed in all the gay and radiant colours of hope and happiness; but, on the contrary, it was exhibited as the most fatal and melancholy of human passions. With the strange wayward delight of the young heart ere it has known actual sorrow, she seemed to riot and revel amid death and woe, laying prostrate hope, life, and affection. Of all the episodical tales introduced into the general design of the principal poem, not one but terminated fearfully or sorrowfully: the heroine herself was the fading victim of crossed and wasted affections. The shorter poems which filled up the volume, and which were, mostly, of extreme beauty, were still based on the wrecks and agonies of humanity.

It might be imagined that this morbid indulgence of so strong an appetite for grief was but the first dipping of the playful foot in the sunny shallows of that flood of mortal experience through which all have to pass, and but the dallying, yet desperate, pleasure afforded by the mingled chill and glittering eddies of the waters which might hereafter swallow up the passer-through, and that the first real pang of actual pain would scare her youthful fancy into the bosom of those hopes and fascinations with which the young mind is commonly only too much delighted to surround itself. But it is a singular fact that, spite of her own really cheerful disposition, and spite of all the advice of her most influential friends, she persisted in this tone from the first to the last of her works, from that hour to the hour of her lamented death. Her poems, though laid in scenes and times capable of any course of events, and though filled to overflowing with the splendour and gauds and high-toned sentiments of chivalry, though enriched with all the colours and ornaments of a most fertile and sportive fancy, were still but the heralds and delineations of melancholy, misfortune, and death. Let anyone turn to any, or all, of her poetical volumes, and say whether this be not so, with few, and, in most of them, no exceptions. The very words of her first heroine might have literally been uttered as her own :—

> Sad were my shades ; methinks they had
>   Almost a tone of prophecy—
> I ever had from earliest youth
>   A feeling what my fate would be.
>
> *The Improvisatrice*, p. 3.

This is one singular peculiarity of the poetry of L. E. L. ; and her poetry must be confessed to be peculiar. It is entirely her own. It had one prominent and fixed character, and that character belonged solely to itself. The rhythm, the feeling, the style and phraseology of L. E. L.'s poetry, were such that you could immediately recognise it, though the writer's name was not mentioned. Love was still the great theme, and misfortune the great doctrine. It was not the less remarkable that she retained to the last the poetical tastes of her very earliest years. The themes of chivalry and romance, feudal pageants and Eastern splendour, delighted her imagination as much in the full growth as in the budding of her genius.

L'ENVOI

Farewell, farewell ! Thy latest word is spoken ;
  The lute thou lov'dst hath given its latest tone ;
Yet not without a lingering, parting token
  Hast thou gone from us, young and gifted one !
And what in love thou gavest, here we treasure,
  Sweet words of song penned in those far-off wilds,
And pure and righteous thoughts, in lofty measure,
  Strong as a patriot's, gentle as a child's.

Here shrine we them, like holy relics keeping,
  That they who loved thee may approach and read ;
May know thy latest thoughts ; may joy in weeping
  That thou wast worthy to be loved indeed !
Farewell, farewell ! And as thy heart could cherish,
  For love, a flower, the sere leaf of a tree,—
So from these pages shall not lightly perish
  Thy latest lays—memento flowers of thee !

MARY HOWITT.

This once celebrated poetess, the daughter of an army agent, was born in London in 1802. At a very early age she began to write for the magazines of the day, and when the 'Annuals' were published, she became a constant contributor to their pages. Her most important poems are 'The Improvisatrice,' 'The Troubadour,' 'The Zenana,' 'The Golden Violet,' and 'The Vow of the Peacock.' She also wrote a few novels, and for several years was editor of 'Fisher's Drawing-room Scrap-book,' a work which had a very large sale. She always wrote under, and was known by, her initials, L. E. L.

In June 1838 she married Mr. George Maclean, and shortly afterwards accompanied him to Cape Coast Castle—a wretched, unhealthy place on the west coast of Africa—of which Maclean was governor. In the winter of the same year, her friends in London—and she had very many—were shocked by the announcement of her death on October 5, from the effects of an overdose of prussic acid ! Why or by whom administered, no one of her friends ever knew.

THE COUNTESS OF BLESSINGTON

MARGARET POWER, the daughter of an Irish squire of Curragheen, co. Waterford, was born there on September 1, 1789. Her father treated her very harshly, and when only fifteen years of age she was glad to escape from him and marry a Captain Palmer, who died in 1817. In the following year she became the wife of the Earl of Blessington, who, to her great delight, took her to travel on the Continent, where a great part of her early life was spent, and where her great beauty and her intellectual gifts made her distinguished in fashionable and literary society.

Unfortunately Lord Blessington died in 1829. His widow then returned to London, where she was cheered by the companionship of her sister Ellen, who was married to Viscount Canterbury. When her affairs were put in order, Lady Blessington settled at Gore House, Kensington, where for fourteen years she was the leader of literary and artistic society, in which she was assisted by her late husband's nephew, Count D'Orsay, a portrait-artist of much merit, and by her nieces, the two Misses Power. Lady Blessington wrote many books that were successful :—' The Magic Lantern,' 'The Idler in France,' 'The Idler in Italy,' 'The Confessions of an Elderly Gentleman,' and 'The Confessions of an Elderly Lady,' 'The Governess,' 'The Belle of a Season,' and many others. But she was best known as the editor of 'The Keepsake' and 'The Book of Beauty,' for which she enlisted the talents of all the great writers of the day, including Lord Byron and Sir Walter Scott. Her soirées were attended and crowded by literary men of eminence and noted artists, and in her way she was a little queen of society ; but Lady Blessington was over-ambitious and much too sanguine. She had an income of 3,000*l.* a year, but, expecting that her literary labours would make up the balance, she spent over 4,000*l.* Mr. Charles Heath died, owing her a considerable sum, and poor Lady Blessington was obliged to leave her beautiful house at Kensington, which had been decorated with presents from her many admirers, and take refuge in Paris, where ill-health and trouble soon caused her death, on June 4, 1849.

Count D'Orsay designed, and her friends erected, a tomb to her memory in Père la Chaise.

THE RIVER LOIRE AND THE CITY OF TOURS

By J. C.

The Loire, one of the largest, is perhaps the most beautiful of the rivers of France. Unlike the swiftly-flowing and tumultuous Rhone, the Loire, from its source in the Cevennes Mountains in the far-distant department of Ardèche, flows tranquilly through half France, passing the towns of Nevers, Orleans, Blois, Tours, Angers, and Nantes; with numerous chateaux and villages upon its banks, which are so richly covered with vineyards, orchards, and cornfields that parts of this country have for ages been known as the 'Garden of France.' After receiving many tributaries, the chief of which are the Allier and Vienne, this majestic river reaches the Bay of Biscay, 600 miles from its source. At times it overflows its banks and causes much destruction, and after a hot and rainless summer the bed of the stream becomes very narrow and is covered with numerous islets and sand banks.

At Tours it is very wide, and is spanned by a magnificent bridge of fifteen arches. This city is a favourite resort of English people, who find it more economical to live there than at home. The cathedral is a very fine building, with a noble stained-glass window and a beautifully carved marble monument to the two children of Charles VIII. and Anne of Brittany. The other important buildings are modern, for the city was wrecked at the time

of the Revolution, when the fine old Church of St. Martin of Tours, except the tower, was also destroyed. One of the chief places of interest is the establishment of Messrs. Mâme, the celebrated printers and publishers of missals and school books for the Church. Very different is it in its surroundings to the places of business of the London printers. We enter through a gateway into an imposing quadrangle, in the middle of which is a fountain constantly playing; round the paved courtyard are large boxes filled with oleanders and orange-trees, and the general air of peace and quietness strikes the visitor. The interior of the building corresponds: everything is arranged with the greatest care, and one envies even the clerks in the counting-house of this model workshop.

The drawing from which Mr. R. Wallis made the accompanying charming engraving was one of the series produced in 'Turner's Annual Tour' in 1832, when the great painter, with Mr. Leitch Ritchie as a companion, visited the principal cities on the Loire.

www.ingramcontent.com/pod-product-compliance
Lightning Source LLC
Chambersburg PA
CBHW021820230426
43669CB00008B/812